The Total Sports Experience
—for Kids

The Total Sports Experience
—*for Kids*

A Parents' Guide to Success in Youth Sports

AUBREY H. FINE, ED.D., AND
MICHAEL L. SACHS, PH.D.

Foreword by Luc Robitaille

Illustrations by Carmen Lindsay and Eva Sachs

Diamond Communications, Inc.
South Bend, Indiana
1997

The Total Sports Experience—*for Kids*
Copyright © 1997 byAubrey H. Fine, Ed.D. and
Michael L. Sachs, Ph.D.

10 9 8 7 6 5 4 3 2 1

Manufactured in the United States of America

Diamond Communications, Inc.
Post Office Box 88
South Bend, Indiana 46624-0088
Editorial: (219) 299-9278
Orders Only: 1-800-480-3717
Fax: (219) 299-9296

Library of Congress Cataloging-in-Publication Data

Fine, Aubrey H.
    The total sports experience--for kids : a parent's guide to
success in youth sports / Aubrey H. Fine and Michael L.
Sachs ; foreword by Luc Robitaille ; illustrations by
Carmen Lindsay and Eva Sachs.
        p.   cm.
    Includes bibliographical references (p.).
    ISBN 1-888698-06-3
    1. Sports for children. 2. Parent and child. 3. Sports-
-Psychological aspects. I. Sachs, Michael L. II. Title.
GV709.2.F53   1997
796' .083--dc21
                                                    96-45052
                                                        CIP

Table of Contents

Dedication

Aubrey:

To Sean and Corey—The boys in my life, who have given me the opportunity to celebrate with them their joy and love of sport.

This book is also dedicated to many other influential individuals. I would like to acknowledge the many young athletes whom I have observed over the years who have demonstrated the true spirit and lessons taught through sports. To Nate, Danny, Eric, Matt, Dustin, Nick, Noel, and Kevin—this book is a tribute to your perseverance, determination, and enthusiasm you have revealed through your devotion to the game.

To coaches, such as Pete, Don, Punky, Mike, John, and Keith who have given generously of their time to help children reach their potential and fulfill their dreams.

Finally, this book is dedicated to all the families we have been blessed with meeting through sports. To the Bauers and the Hansons, (and to many other families we would love to acknowledge)—thanks for the greatest gift that these experiences have cast upon us: friendship.

Michael:

To Rachel and Emily—may all your sporting experiences be enormously fun and successful. Carpe diem!

Acknowledgments

There are many people we would like to thank for helping us in the development of this book and bringing it to fruition. Our first thanks go to Jill Langford, Sharon Hill, and the rest of the staff at Diamond Communications for their support, encouragement, and patience. We would also like to thank our colleagues for their assistance, in particular Brad Cardinal, Kate Hays, Jack Lesyk, David Pargman, Ann Thomas, and John Scolinos, who provided feedback on several chapters and gave us much-needed guidance. Thanks also to our students who assisted in collecting surveys for Chapter 7: Jennifer Baker, Deborah DiLiberto-Mazda, and Anne Pribulka Cutler, as well as Robert Ciervo and Shawn Gomer, who provided suggestions on illustrations for the book. We would also like to thank Jim Nice and Pat Brisson from Reich, Brisson and Reich Hockey Group for their assistance in aiding in the communication with Mr. Robitaille in preparing the foreword for the book. Last, but certainly not least, thanks to our families for their support—Nya and Fay, Sean, Corey, Rachel, and Emily.

Foreword

It is a great privilege to have the opportunity to write the foreword for this excellent resource. I strongly believe that this book will become an invaluable reference for all parents who have children in organized sports. Several summers ago, while I was living in L.A. (playing hockey with the L.A. Kings), I was involved with a youth hockey camp called "Skate with the Pros." It was during that period that I met Dr. Fine and became acquainted with his philosophy of sports and children. I am strongly convinced that you will also be impressed with his and Dr. Sachs' insights on how parents can help make sporting activities rewarding for their children.

As a professional athlete, I often find myself talking to children and their parents about sports. I constantly encourage parents to let their children go out and have fun. That is why children should participate. In fact, I have always felt that if you lose that joyous feeling, the sport is no longer a game.

As a child, I was fortunate enough to have a father who was very supportive. He always seemed to enjoy watching my games, and never seemed mad or discouraged about the outcome. He felt his job was to help me secure opportunities which I desired. He also felt that just being there was what he really needed to do. In looking back at my childhood, I can honestly say how grateful I am that my father was constantly encouraging. I was often pretty hard on myself during my early years as a youth hockey player. Not only was my dad encouraging and supportive, he would always try to listen. I remember fondly him saying to me, "If you give 100% of yourself, that is all that is important. If you did the best you could!" This is exactly the message that Aubrey and Michael share with you in this book. This is a key element of this wonderful volume.

The Total Sports Experience—*for Kids*

I find that both Aubrey and Michael have been very insightful in clarifying the role of parents in youths' sport. They have provided an overview of why sports are important to a child, and how parents can help children become successful. They provide a wonderful explanation of what is success and how parents can help support their child.

Each of the chapters builds on the previous chapter's conclusions. The writers provide a direction that families can put into place to help their children have a rich, challenging, and enjoyable experience. Attention has been given to explain the range of opportunities that are available to children, including those children who are extremely talented as well as challenged.

The authors also focus on numerous other elements that are crucial for parents to appreciate. These include the steps that should be considered in selecting a sport for a child, an understanding of the differences between competitive and cooperative sports, and a recognition of how healthy self-esteem influences performance. I found the chapters on how to select a coach as well the chapter on strategies to enhance performance very informative. There is even a chapter summarizing what children expressed in interviews on what they really wanted from their parents in sports. This information is quite revealing. The following chapter that is intended for children to give to parents is one I feel can be shared with any child! It's simple and great!

As a professional athlete, I recognize the pressure one has to perform at a high level. However, I have always felt that pressure to perform from parents usually makes it even harder for a child. I strongly believe that the greatest gift parents can give their children is to be there for the youngster—for the good as well as the bad. When I was a child, I would often be discouraged after my team lost an important match. My father always tried to impart a message that everyone needs to put in the proper perspective. *In the end, win or lose, it is just a game.*

Foreword

I know that all of you will find this book to be very useful and inspiring while your children are involved in organized sports. Remember, it is your child's game. Let the children enjoy their accomplishments and challenges. Be there when things are not always positive, and help your children learn to be the best they can. But most of all, help your children realize that the most important dimension is sheer joy and fun. That is the greatest gift the game can give back to children.

So open your eyes for a fresh perspective on your child's game. I am certain the book will enhance your outlook. Remember, in the end, the years you invest in your child's sporting activities will all be memories. Cherish this time today. Share your child's game and enjoy the splendor of the quest.

Luc Robitaille
New York Rangers
July 1996

Chapter 1

The Road Well Traveled:

Sports and Childhood The Flavorful Journey of Children

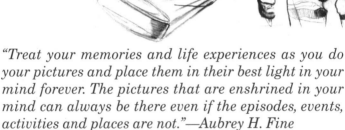

"Treat your memories and life experiences as you do your pictures and place them in their best light in your mind forever. The pictures that are enshrined in your mind can always be there even if the episodes, events, activities and places are not."—Aubrey H. Fine

(adapted from the quote from Jennie Jerome Churchill: "Treat your friends as you do your pictures and place them in their best light.")

We are about to start on a great adventure that will allow us to be observers and celebrate the accomplishments of our children. Over the years, our endeavors will take us to many places. We will make many new friends; others families will become extensions of our own; and the memories of athletic contests will be cherished for a lifetime.

Our trip with our children will take us to many places. We may find ourselves active in organizing league play. Our children's involvement may encourage us to volunteer in numerous roles. We will also spend hundreds of hours helping our children refine their skills. We will drive many hours to games and practices at all hours of the day and evening. Our voices may become hoarse from cheering for our favorite teams. We may find ourselves, at times, shedding tears as our children experience disappointments. However, what we must begin to accept is that while we may choose to become actively involved in our children's activities, as observers, we must recognize that our role is that of spectators and supporters. It is the children who own the events.

This will be an important dimension of our book. We should be supporting and involved in our children's lifestyles. After all, we are only parents to young children and teens for a short while (although at times it may not feel that way). We must appreciate our roles and know our place. We hope that, after reading this book, parents will begin to get a better appreciation of the importance of sports in their children's lives and recognize that their support, love, and respect are part of the driving force that sustains their children. Although this will be a primary message throughout the book, the chapters will build upon each other, giving insight to many critical elements of youth sports (i.e., selecting a sport, identifying the most appropriate level, selecting a coach, enhancing performance on and off the playing field, and, finally, what children want you to know about their games).

So, where do we begin? Is there a classic image of a child at play? Depending on the season of the year, the age, and even the region of the country, the activities may differ, but the zest and the tenacity to play do not. In fact, over the generations, while the venues may have changed, and the equipment has become updated, the sounds and sights are pretty much the same as they have always been.

Children at play! Words do not give justice to the magnificence that is unveiled by that phrase. Children are the living, breathing custodians of sports, and their passion for all games is real. Families put together scrapbooks and fill closets with photograph albums, videos, trophies, and medals that are collections of treasures of the past. These home depositories are occupied with memories filled with moments of joy and perhaps sadness. They represent a history and a chronology of childhood, neatly packaged and featured. As parents, many would like to have the chance to relive these moments, but instead we must settle for the recorded memories. Why are these memories so important? Are they a reflection of some of the major milestones of childhood? What are they filled with?

It hits them the moment they awake. What is going to be the game-winning play? Some children fantasize about being the MVP, while others may be mentally rehearsing their swing, their kick, their catch. The obsession may be so significant that they become distracted from their regular daily activities. Every moment of any given day, there are children holding on to a vision about making it to the big leagues. Is that why children play? Are they there to fulfill their dreams, to build their dreams, or simply to live life to the fullest? What is exciting is the fact that for each child who plays, the ambitions are different. That is what is so appealing in our world of tremendous diversity.

The game-day pilgrimage to the ballfield is filled with the sounds of children actively pursuing their dreams. Their souls are awakened and take flight with the power of the energy within them. This is their game and they will try to hold on to it forever. The day will come when they will be in the stands cheering on their children and the sons and daughters of their friends and other family members, but today is their day. Before organized sports take over, or perhaps at different stages in each child's life, children will be responsible for regulating their games. The sandlots, the backyard rinks, the corner basketball courts will be their kingdom. There will be no referees, no coaches, usually no captains. They just play and, in most cases, they do so quite successfully. Children usually learn to sort things out for themselves. Sure, there will be occasional arguments and fights, but in the end, together, they will determine their own rules. Sometimes things will not turn out the way they wanted, but they will persevere. In informal sports, children learn to be fair. They seem to experience the world through play. It is the game they seek out; the joy of playing and the excitement they will experience are the major objectives.

Some may question at what point this zest fades away, and the childishness disappears. Some people believe that the childish enthusiasm never really ends. For adults, playing sports with tenacity and love may represent a link to their past.

Ken Dryden, legendary goaltender for the Montreal Canadiens, wrote in his book, *Home Game*, "When I was a kid, I just played. In September the equipment came out and in arenas and backyards the games began: one practice, two games a week; at lunch time, from school-end until dinner, Saturdays, Sundays, and holidays from morning to floodlit night..... The pattern and shape of my years, and the seasons passed. From September to March to September again, until someday some coach, burying his chin in his chest, would mutter, 'Sorry son, maybe next year.' And it would be over. I kept expecting this would happen, but it never did, and I saw no reason to stop."

The Road Well Traveled

As an adult, Dryden became one of the greatest goaltenders in hockey history. He played for the famous Montreal Canadiens in the '70s. When he retired from professional sports, he eventually returned to the game he loved. Now, he pays his weekly ice fees and plays pick-up games with his friends. There are no referees, and no coaches who potentially will tell him or any of his teammates that they are not good enough and need to go home. It is almost as good as childhood, but it will never be the same.

The outcome for Dryden and many adults is the same. In some ways, the journey through sports can be explained as a cycle of life. It begins with the child as a player who eventually becomes an adult. As players age, they have to accept roles as fans or observers. Nevertheless, one thing is certain: the game continues. The only major difference is that the players' faces and names change. Every day, the carousel ride ends for one child, but another child takes that vacant place. For most children, all that will remain when the ride is over are memories of the activities that filled their childhood. Hopefully, the memories will be rich with success and joy. That is not to say that disappointments will be avoidable. However, what we can hope to avoid for the children of tomorrow are recollections that are disturbed because of adults who interfered and took their games away!

Definition—Leisure

The concept of leisure is intimately related to the cultural context that it is used. Leisure came to use through the Latin word *licere*, which means "to be permitted." The French refined the term and developed the word *loisir*, meaning "free time." The word leisure virtually means exception or permission as applied to an opportunity. Some believe that leisure is the opportunity to do nothing. The action of doing nothing does not describe an emptiness, but rather an occasion for self-reflection. Leisure is much more than occupying oneself in free time.

Productive leisure time experiences definitely become critical dimensions of an individual's lifestyle.

Theories Explaining Why Children Play in Sports

There are three theories of interest here—Piagetian theory, Social Learning theory, and Arousal theory. Each of the theories provides a different position on why children play in sports. Each has a different school of thought and interprets play from a unique perspective. None of the three completely explains play. However, together they seem to answer portions of why children may play in sport.

Developmental psychologists believe that sport allows children to enhance their cognitive, emotional, and physical development. Through play, children learn to expand their horizons and challenge themselves to grow. Piagetian theory explains four major stages of development. Piaget saw play as an area in which children can refine their developing skills. Furthermore, Piagetian developmental theory also explains why certain children are not developmentally ready to be involved in certain complex sports (e.g., sports with rules, or, for that matter, other competitive activities). For example, children need to learn how to cooperate with others before they are challenged in team sports to be competitive with others.

Behaviorists, proponents of learning theory, characterize play and sport involvement as a behavior that is learned, just like any other activity. Play serves as a means for learning about the social world. This behavioral theoretical orientation assumes that playing in sports is a learned behavior. The theory points out that children who are successful in a certain activity may play because they feel rewarded or reinforced. On the other hand, a child who fails at a given play activity will not continue to engage in that sport because the failure is linked to punishment, and punished behavior is not repeated. It seems apparent that most children engage in activities at which they do well.

Social learning theory points out that children may play and learn sports from watching others. They may find themselves modeling or simply copying the actions of others. Children may find the results of watching certain sports or athletes rewarding or reinforcing and therefore are urged to follow in their heroes' footsteps. This would explain why children try to emulate Magic Johnson, Michael Jordan, Eric Lindros, and Wayne Gretzky. Registration numbers in certain youth sports are sometimes dependent on the growth of the sport's professional activity. Children try to copy their heroes' feats of accomplishment and are excited about playing.

Social learning theory also points out that children will learn about sport from watching and integrating the lessons of others. When they see peers perform an act and get rewarded, they will often try to duplicate the act. The same occurs in reverse when children watch their teammates make decisions or they receive negative feedback. They are more likely to try not to copy that behavior.

Finally, some believe that children play in sports because the behavior is motivated by the need to elevate the level of arousal of the body. Those who follow this belief system (arousal theory) suggests that children play in sports because of the need to stay aroused. It is stimulus-seeking behavior. Sport participation provides stimulation because it is concerned with characteristics that are associated with stimulation—namely, novelty, uncertainty, and complexity.

The Value of Leisure and Sports

Play is not only enjoyable, but also a serious and significant pursuit of children. Some believe that if we want to understand children, we need to take time to understand their play. Play represents a key to opening up doors of life. While playing, children discover the roots of their civilization, learn how things work, enhance their abilities to solve problems, and learn how to interact and socialize with others. One of the cornerstones of the study of play is that when children are at play, they are, by definition, engaged in an experience that is inherently meaningful. The meaning and rationale of the activity do not have to be obvious to the child.

Research points out that recreation and leisure fill significant needs in many people's lives. A consensus of some of the research indicates that leisure satisfaction is a principal source of perceived quality of life. Meaningful participation in sports and leisure can be tremendously helpful in reducing feelings of helplessness. We agree that positive recreational experiences in general, and involvement in quality sporting activities in particular can contribute to a person's sense of self-efficacy and empowerment. For example, the child who joins a team and is made to feel welcome and valuable will eventually feel like an important link on the team. Such an experience could have a monumental impact on the child. The sense of belonging and feeling wanted can strengthen the way children view themselves. Another example could be a child who is involved in any martial arts program. The outcome of this experience has been noted by many as an avenue to enhance self-discipline and self-concept.

Perhaps the most important dimension of participating in sports, or any leisure experience, is that of perceived freedom and perceived autonomy. To get the full value of this aspect, children must feel that they have choices before participating. When a child feels forced to participate in a specific sport, or does not want to play, this dimension is tremendously influenced, because the child's sense of perceived freedom and choice may have been ignored. The child may feel pressured to play and will eventually want to give up.

Sports participation seems to offer one of the best opportunities for children of all ages to experience a sense of self-determination because it really does offer a chance for an individual to be in control. Leisure participation also offers individuals opportunities to demonstrate mastery and competence over activities. Finally, sporting activities provide an escape from everyday personal and interpersonal environments. The experience of participating in sports can be used as an opportunity to set aside issues and difficulties and engage in activities that are enjoyable and personally satisfying.

Participating in leisure is not only the actual involvement. Leisure is about life; it has to do with choices, interactions, and freedom. Play and learning are truly bound together. Aristotle said that learning is pleasurable, and one could say that learning is play. Constructive play activities put the child in the driver's seat and through these experiences the child can become much more of an active learner. Through play and sports, children acquaint themselves with sets of realities, both inner and outer, and learn how to satisfy their needs and those of others. Play magically transforms children into anything they desire—from a super basketball player to a clown in the circus. Through play and sports, the obstacles facing children can be reduced. Consequently, children who are not well coordinated still can dream about being marathon runners and uncovering some of the treasures of the universe.

The Moral Value of Sports: What is Homeplate?

To begin our discussion of how sports mold the moral characters of young athletes, we will use a concrete object to help formulate a clear picture. When you think of homeplate in baseball, what is conjured up in your mind? What is homeplate? Why is it called homeplate? Why is it shaped differently from all of the other bases? What does it represent in the game and perhaps figuratively? Does it represent the ultimate goal of any team: scoring and winning?

In doing research for this book, we found it fascinating that, although the physical structure of the game changes as the participants get older (for example, the distance between bases is lengthened, the bats become heavier), and expectations increase, the size of the bases does not. The size of homeplate never changes: it stays 17-inches wide at all levels of play. The same phenomenon is also noted in other sports, including the size of hockey and soccer nets and the height of basketball hoops.

However, we chose to illustrate homeplate because of what it represents. When you turn the base around, it looks just like a house. A home is where many tenets of social behavior and morals are established. Does homeplate figuratively represent a physical space where many of our values can be strengthened and practiced? Do sports provide children with an avenue for constructively developing and fostering moral growth?

We have seen a tremendous change over the past few decades in the way in which children are supported and parented. The children of the '90s have many more challenges and difficulties than did previous generations. Has homeplate changed for them? Simply answered, yes it has. Children of the '90s are faced with numerous obstacles that have made growing up a greater challenge. There are many factors which have definitely affected the emotional stability of our youth. Some of them are: a higher rate of divorce in the '90s (more in the United States than any other country in the world), blended and single-parent families, latchkey children, the impact of child care on our youth, media, gangs, and the proliferation and addiction to various legal and illegal substances.

What does a quality sports life contribute to our children? In many ways, the values and beliefs that are necessary to engage in productive living are dealt with on a microscopic scale in sports. The values that are necessary to be a law-abiding citizen who is also driven, motivated, and concerned are all taught in sports. The foundation of the homeplate could represent the development of important moral and humanistic traits that help children become winners on and off the field. Although the apex of homeplate is very small, it may represent the roof that holds it all together. In this context, widening homeplate would only weaken its structure.

When you think about it, widening our moral values and making excuses for bad behavior only make our living climate less positive. It is the same in sports! Excusing negativity or lack of will to perform, just because a child has the skill, is extremely unfortunate. Look at professional athletes who have become poor role models to our children. Although they have tremendous physical talent, some have tried to widen their homeplate because of the exceptions they feel they deserve. For some athletes, social and moral conduct, on and off the playing field, leaves much to be desired. In making exceptions in order to retain their talent on a team, some teams have suffered.

The following two sections will expand on our idea of homeplate and will continue our discussion of how sports involvement influences children. We will show by example how experiences teach children about who they are and how they can become better people.

The Lessons That are Taught in Play and Sports
The proposition that sports build character is believed by many people. Parents are frequently advised to enroll their

children in a sporting activity because of its related benefits. We often recommend that parents enroll their children in various sporting venues. We frequently highlight the benefits that we view as outcomes from sports participation: making friends, stress reduction, and many other productive social experiences are just a few worthy of note. Sometimes we are cautious, and encourage parents to assess the programs that they are considering. We suggest they review their children's needs, as well as the demands that are placed on the children. We will discuss these specific concerns in the following chapter.

Over the years many have attempted to investigate the influence of organized sports experiences on building social character and other appropriate prosocial behaviors. Although the research suggests that sports participation can help build character, it does not automatically do so. Indeed, sometimes sports is said to build *characters*, individuals who engage in behaviors that are not acceptable within society's normative values. However, there are numerous social benefits that children can gain through productive sporting alternatives.

All children have certain needs met in sports. Their choices of activities may differ, but their goals are universal. The internal satisfaction that children gain from playing appears to be the greatest gain. To get children to want to be involved, they must enjoy themselves. This must be the most important goal! Children want to enjoy their free time either by playing games, or being involved in sports with peers. When the joy is not there, children feel cheated. Having fun is the key element here.

An indirect benefit which children experience from participation is the development of skills that relate to their social adjustment and development. Making friends and reaffirming friendships are very important to children. In general, playing on a sports team allows children to learn and practice getting along. To be effective teammates, children have to learn to work with each other. Later in this chapter more examples will be given to highlight team building; for now, an example will illustrate the position.

Years ago, one of us (Aubrey) had the opportunity to work with boys in a community setting. Many of the boys had emotional problems and they were constantly fighting. They were trying to field an intramural basketball team, but the boys could not work together. Either they would argue among themselves or they would become one-person teams. Discouraged by this behavior, I shouted, "Everyone, look at your hands!" The team was surprised into silence by this seemingly insane request. Now I had to quickly think of something to say before I lost their attention. "If I cut away your palms," I continued, "what would you do with your fingers?" The boys observed that nothing could be done with their fingers, since the palm keeps the fingers together and makes them work. Slowly, the boys began to discuss how fortunate they were that all of their bodily functions were in order. Some of them related stories about individuals who had disabilities and how difficult they thought it was for them. Eventually, we arrived at the desired discussion point. A team, like the palms of our hands, is what keeps individuals working together. A team that is disjointed is one that is ineffective. It also would be an unpleasant experience.

Just as a palm gets the fingers to work in unison, so does a team with its members. One goal of sports in general is not only to work on individual social adjustment but also to allow children to become more comfortable in working and interacting with each other. As years go by, this primary objective is reduced. However, if a child continues to struggle with the members of a team, this issue may eventually grow; it could become the weak link of a team. Over the years, both of us have dealt with teams that had all the necessary talent but could not work together. A team that is not united will struggle due to the internal perils and disputes!

Probably the most basic benefit from sports participation is its contribution to healthier physical and motor development. Regular participation in exercise and sports helps children develop all major physical systems of the body, particularly the cardiovascular system, and strong muscles and bones. There are many physiological effects of regular participation, and each sport affects different systems of the body to greater or lesser degrees. For example, soccer and swimming will have a greater impact on the cardiovascular system than will baseball or gymnastics; however, gymnastics will have much greater benefits for strength and flexibility than baseball, and so on. The key factor is for children to participate.

Tied in to physical development is motor skill development. All sports involve motor skills, from the basic strokes required in swimming to the complex movements required in baseball (eye-hand coordination, movement patterns in fielding and throwing to a base, in sliding correctly, etc.). Participating in sports will help develop these motor skills and help refine the kinesthetic (bodily) awareness that comes from movement.

In addition to these many benefits, there are specific lessons that sports can teach us. One way of looking at these lessons is presented in the following section.

The Eight Essential Lessons of Sports: Wisdom for Growth

Years ago we had the good fortune of meeting a baseball coach named John Scolinos. John is nationally regarded as an outstanding college baseball coach. During the Summer Olympics held in Los Angeles in 1984, Scolinos was the pitching coach for the USA Olympic baseball team. Over his career, he has had an impact on the lives of many young people and their parents, as well as on many others on and off the field. John has always recognized that sports involvement has as much to do with the game as it does with life in general. He has lectured nationally on his beliefs about how sports involvement strengthens character and widens the quality of opportunities that athletes experience. We are going to take the liberty of paraphrasing and, to some extent, modifying some of his principles (with his permission). As a whole, each of these elements relates to character building, which, indirectly, is probably the greatest element that productive sports will affect. Through positive competition, children learn about themselves and potentially recognize that they are more capable and stronger than they thought they were.

Lesson 1—Learning to cope with failure. Coach John Wooden once said, "Do not let what you cannot do interfere with what you can do." Children will be exposed to situations on a daily basis where they will be confronted with failure. They will have to learn that they will have to defeat failure by overcoming it. Within sports, children are exposed to the prospect of failure in a variety of ways.

As team members, they will be exposed to team failures. Although not as personal, they will have to recognize their impact and develop strategies that can help them and their teammates overcome. Teams that cannot accept failure will have difficulty reaching for success. Unfortunately, failure, at times, brings out the worst in people. Some children may want to blame failures on others, but teams must remain united through the good and the bad. On the other hand, children also have to accept their personal setbacks and realize that failure may only be a postponement of victory. They should not deny themselves ownership of a problem, and must learn to prevail. Children have to realistically challenge themselves and make goals that can help them achieve. Setting unrealistic goals will increase the possibility of bouts with discouragement and a sense of failure.

On the flip side of failure is learning to accept success with grace. Children need to respect their challenges and work toward excellence. Successful teams may become overconfident with their skills, and begin to fail. Many a professional coach has noted that it is sometimes harder to keep teams motivated and working hard when they have won the league's top award (i.e., Lombardi trophy, the Stanley Cup, etc.). All of us would agree that we would be happier achieving success rather than failure. Nevertheless, what is important to point out is that, through sports, children can be challenged to overcome adversity and become successful. Having an opportunity to achieve success and overcome failure are two elements of meaningful character building.

Lesson 2—Developing a sense of commitment. The old cliché "there is no such thing as a free lunch" is a lesson that is emphasized in sports. To get better, or, for that matter, to get what they aspire to, children have to develop a sense of responsibility and a commitment to the game. That means when the game begins, children must begin to see that they have to be ready to play. Commitment to excellence also requires that one has to make an effort to self-improve. Teams are built with athletes who are committed every day. Teammates depend on each other. If only some of the team shows up ready to play, a missing link could be fatal.

What does commitment mean? It represents a covenant among athletes and their goals that apply to an entire team. Without a commitment, especially as they age, children will falter in sports, because they neglect to address the key ingredient that unlocks many doors. The desire and commitment need to be clear. As Michael Jordan elegantly suggests, "The game is my wife. It demands loyalty and responsibility, and it gives me back fulfillment and peace." Children have to be committed to their teams, and to their performance.

Lesson 3—Handling fear. Everything that is new can cause some fear. Participation in sports can help children eliminate two types of fears. The first sense of fear relates to failure and all the issues that we discussed in Lesson 2. However, within sports, children are challenged to learn new things that could provoke some fear. For an example, when a Little Leaguer goes up to bat, he or she may have to get over being afraid of being hit by the ball. This type of fear is possible in any sport. Another fear that children have to learn to overcome is the fear of making a mistake. Sometimes when people fear making a mistake, they tighten up and their performance decreases.

Lesson 4—Handling frustration. Probably the hardest thing for all of us to overcome is handling frustrating outcomes. Frustrations can be elicited in many circumstances. Children can be frustrated by their own performance, or the team's performance. Children can become frustrated with the coaching they receive, or with their teammates. Learning to overcome frustration by acting appropriately versus developing a defeated attitude is what children need to do. Unfortunately, these frustrations can make or break a positive experience. A character-building lesson that is gained from handling frustrations is perseverance and learning to adjust to undesirable outcomes.

Lesson 5—Being part of the team. Children learn very early in their lives the importance of team building. In all sports, children experience the important lessons that being part of a team promotes. Through sports, children can learn to be selfless rather than selfish. Sports can teach children that they will have to sometimes sacrifice individual needs for the good of the team. A team filled with superstars who are not willing to work together will eventually fail.

Through sports and effective mentoring, children can learn to develop problem solving and conflict mediation skills, and they can learn the importance of being contributors. To illustrate this, we will provide an example explaining the different types of children who play sports. Basically, teams consist of three types of individuals: the athlete, the competitor, and the link.

The first type of player is the athlete. This is the child who possesses all the requisite talent, and, with the right circumstances, can be an outstanding asset to any team. However, coaches and teammates never know when this child will show up and really play. Just because players have the skills does not mean that they will be productive. The child's motivation to aspire as well as his/her attitudes are two important elements.

The second type of child is the competitor. These children are hard working, but only care about themselves. Their efforts are only initiated for their own benefit. Although being a competitor is generally considered to be a positive attribute, in this case it is also a significant weakness. A team of talented youngsters who do not pull together will not have a distinct force.

The last type of child is the link. The child who is the link is one who attempts to put the team first. This is the child who will put out more energy trying to get the team to work together. Links may learn to sacrifice their personal needs so that others will come through. The linking child is one who will try to run interference and motivate teammates.

All teams need players who are true athletes, and a team without any talent, although filled with children who are all links, may not be the strongest in the league standings. However, most coaches will agree that they would be willing to yield some talent and select kids who are more linkers and doers. These are the children who will turn losing squads into winners. They do this by understanding that linking a team will make the team stronger.

Lesson 6—Handling embarrassment. Most successful people would agree they have had to learn to handle embarrassing situations. Being an athlete involves learning to handle situations and contend with difficulties. All of us recognize how awkward it must be for a child to strike out, to drop the ball in football and baseball, or allow an easy goal in hockey or soccer. However, all of these outcomes are a natural part of a game. Embarrassing situations will happen, and children have to become resilient and handle difficult situations with grace and good humor.

Lesson 7—Handling competition. Playing sports means you have to handle winning and losing. Later in this book (Chapter 6), we will take a look at psychological skills that will enhance performance. However, for the moment it is relevant to point out that there are some children who seem to handle competition better than others. These are children who develop a competitive edge because they have an inner drive to excel. Is there something else? Athletes must put winning in perspective. Joe Namath, the famous quarterback for the New York Jets, says that at some point in your life you begin to realize you do not have to worry if you don't do everything you are supposed to do right. If you do the best you can, what can worry do for you? You are already doing your best. As we discussed earlier, when children cannot accept their accomplishments, they may have difficulty handling competition.

Lesson 8—Handling adjustments. A challenge that all children have to face in their lives is adjusting. An old English saying suggests that one should "keep company with those who make you better." To get better, one will have to make changes. Adjustments can occur in many situations: adjusting to a new team, adjusting to expectations, adjusting your skills so that you can perform more effectively. Change comes with fine tuning, and for some children the process is quite difficult. However, adjustments are important to accept because they are part of life.

As children age, they will be forced to adjust to many expectations. Sports can possibly get them to experience this process earlier. It can occur in many different situations. Children may have a coach who is not particularly sensitive, or they may move up in a league and need to alter their skills to be successful. These are only a few examples in which children need to adjust their expectations or their approaches so they will handle things more effectively.

Life is full of learning. Children need to be willing to be open to accepting suggestions and trying to implement new strategies into their daily lives. At times, one's competence may be diminished when the adjustments are in their early stage. Players may want to give up because they may doubt themselves. Successfully adjusting to new situations will produce a winner within. Whole societies have vanished because they could not cope with the upheaval of change. There is a lesson that comes from this historical phenomenon. One has to learn at some point to adapt to the demands of one's new future. Sports may promote the goals of this lesson much earlier in life. Children will learn to accept that, with effort, persistence, and fine tuning, they may eventually see the silver lining of success in the clouds of challenges encountered in sports.

Influential Words and Beliefs in Sports:
A Formula for Longevity and Everyday Living

As a complement to the lessons taught through sports, we also want to add our perceptions of statements and words that foster success versus failure. These statements, also an elaboration and modification of the thoughts of John Scolinos, can be impressed on children not only when they play, but in their daily lives as well. Each of these comments represents actions which children need to understand and respect.

1. Five most important words—Surround yourself with good people. In team building, children will begin to appreciate that surrounding themselves with positive role models and people who are contributors is a tremendous asset. Children also need to learn to be compassionate and to support others who are in need of help.

2. Four most important words—Take care of yourself or I can handle it. Children need to realize that they are important people. They must also appreciate their efforts in guarding their sense of self and taking care of their most prized possession—themselves. They need to perceive how important, how precious they are.

The belief system that teaches a child that "I can handle things" allows children to aspire to be the best they can be. A ladder of achievement must include willingness to handle adverse situations before the child can profess that "I did it!" Without the conviction of "I can handle it," children are often left with a belief that they do not know how, they cannot, or they will not.

3. Three most important words—Class, Character, Concern. For children to be successful in life, each of these elements needs to be addressed. Sports not only affect this area, but are influential in it as well. Parents and coaches need to emphasize to children that these are three ingredients that will open up new doors. Children need to have strong character. They must learn to develop empathy and become more interested in the well-being of others.

4. *Two most important words—Thank you or I can.* We have already indirectly discussed the value of the words "I can." Without thinking "I can," a child will probably never reach the top step of a ladder and be able to say "I did." On the other hand, children need to be thankful for the things they receive, both tangibly and emotionally. Being thankful and acknowledging the efforts of others is crucial.

5. *Single most important word—We.* Team building and the importance of being a contributor are all elements invested in "we." When children emphasize "we," they begin to recognize the united strength of others.

Many years ago, Aubrey worked with a group of elite pee wee hockey players. While in the Western USA Regional Championships, he was asked to work with the boys and try to help motivate them. Before games and between periods, the time was spent trying to relax the boys and instill within the team that they got so far not only because of their talent but also because they worked as a team. The understanding of becoming "we" was probably the greatest benefit from their team participation. To help illustrate this principle, Aubrey asked several of the teammates to break a thin strand of rope. The teammates looked bewildered at this ridiculous request, but complied. When all the thin strands were broken, a six-strand entangled rope was presented. When the various players were asked to break this more reinforced rope, they were unable to do so. The rope represented the team. Entangled and committed, they were unbreakable; loosely connected, they would surely weaken under their opponents' assaults. These young athletes understood that as a united group they had tremendous strength. "We" made them winners and the team played splendidly. The final game went into double overtime. The team was finally defeated. Although they were the runners-up in the tournament, they were still winners in their hearts. It is significant that, years later, many of the players remembered our discussion about the ropes. Although they lost a tough battle, they left as winners because they all were part of something—an entity called WE. To commemorate that moment, Aubrey wrote each of the teammates a letter with a small message about "We." On the top of the passage was the title "WE," which consisted not only of two letters but also of strings entangled together.

We

*A Short Story
of Strength and Unity*

*It is through Cooperation, rather than Conflict
that our Greatest Success will originate.
When we coordinate our efforts with the efforts of others,
we will become United and Stronger.
By doing so, we will be more capable of reaching our goals.
There is no such thing as a One Person Team.
A Team will reach it goals only with the help of all its members.
Cooperation, Positive Belief, and Unity builds Success.
You are an Important Strand in our Unbreakable Rope.
You are part of We.*

*A gift presented to all team members of the
L.A. Condors Pee Wee Tier Team, April 1994*

Years after that tournament, I know this message was followed by many of the children on the team. In fact, one of them used portions of the composition as a part of his platform speech for president of his school class. He wanted his classmates to realize that he wanted the student body to unite and energize. They too could become part of a We.

1. Least most important word—I. It is only logical that if "we" was the single most important word that children should appreciate, "I" should be at the opposite end of the spectrum. This is not to say that children should deny their individual goals and achievements. We just want to emphasize that there is no *I* in the word *team*. It is crucial for children to understand that when they play team sports they can not strictly be concerned with their own well-being. This overemphasis may misdirect children's ambitions and they may neglect the importance of being a part of a bigger picture.

2. Two worst words—I quit. Giving up does not teach anything. Children need to learn that they cannot run away from their problems. The opposite of a quitter is a worker, an individual who will not give up. When children say they quit, do they mean quitting a team, quitting because they doubt themselves, or something completely different? The truth is, children need to learn that they have to try and overcome and prevail. They can certainly stop doing anything they do not want to do after careful and logical consideration. Quitting is very different. Quitters leave a place in a very unhappy and discouraged state. Quitters give up and abandon rather than contend with difficulties effectively.

3. Three worst words—I don't care. Commitment is crucial in all of life's events. When people do not care, they paralyze an outcome. If they are not committed to an outcome, the results will inevitably attest to their lack of commitment. Performance is dramatically hampered when children are not invested.

4. Four worst words—Everybody is doing it. Two wrongs do not make a right. Children cannot excuse their behavior just because they believe it is commonly accepted. One should not learn to make excuses, but rather be more accountable for actions. It is unfortunate that many use these four words as excuses for their acts.

5. Five worst words—Let somebody else do it. The world is in need of doers. Someone always has to be a starter. On the other hand, it is always very discouraging to watch children point the finger and say, "let somebody else do it." We all dislike certain activities, but things need to be done, and one cannot pass the buck. Teams are built on contributors rather than those who are self-centered. When a job needs to be done, it is unacceptable to always want to pass it on to others. We are not saying that the load should not be shared equally, but we are strongly convinced that it is inevitable that one should not be dependent on others to do the dirty work! Accountability is crucial.

Why Children Play in Sports

Chapter 7 is devoted to feedback we obtained through interviews conducted with several children on what they did and did not enjoy about sports. However, we would like to highlight some information derived from a study conducted by the American Footwear Association (AFA) in 1991. Within this study, more than 10,000 young people from 11 American cities described how they felt about sports.

The study revealed some fascinating insights from the respondents. Highlights of the study were reported in the popular press including an article in *USA Today* on October 3, 1991.

The AFA prepared a brief brochure in which they published the outcomes from the study. A significant finding was that *winning* is not seen as the major reason why young people

The Total Sports Experience—*for Kids*

Table 1
The 10 Most Important Reasons why
Children Play a School Sport

1. To have fun
2. To improve my skills
3. To stay in shape
4. To do something I'm good at
5. For the excitement
6. To get exercise
7. To play as part of a team
8. For the challenge of competition
9. To learn new skills
10. To win

Table 2
The 11 Most Important Reasons
Children Stop Playing a Sport

1. I lost interest
2. I was not having fun
3. It took too much time
4. Coach was a poor teacher
5. Too much pressure
6. Wanted non-sport activity
7. I was tired of it
8. Needed more time to study
9. Coach played favorites
10. Sport was boring
11. Overemphasis on winning

Table taken from *American Youth and Sports Participation: A Study of 10,000 Students and Their Feelings About Sports*, published in 1991 by the American Footwear Association, 200 Castlewood Drive, North Palm Beach, FL 33408. Reprinted with permission.

continue to play in sports. It seems that having *fun,* improving skills, staying in shape, and experiencing competition are a few of the benefits rated as more important. In fact, it is the joy the children get from the activity that is the most crucial factor in making their decision to remain involved in sports or to drop out. It seems that skill development is even more important to young athletes (even among the best athletes) than winning. Tables 1 and 2 identify the selected choices. Several thousand children in grades 7-12 were used as the source for these responses. Two thousand boys and 1,900 girls in grades 7-12 were used to gather information on what they liked the best, while 2,700 boys and 3,100 girls were polled to explain why they recently stopped playing in sports.

Steven Danish, a professor of Psychology at Virginia Commonwealth University, defined fun (for this study) in sports *"as the quest for balance between challenge and skill. If they are relatively in balance, enjoyment results."* Danish suggests that sports are most rewarding when the child is the definer of the accepted challenge. He goes on to state that when the skills that the child possesses outweigh the challenge the child receives from participating in the selected sport, then the outcome may eventually lead to boredom and possibly dropping out of the sport. On the other hand, when the challenges outweigh the child's skills, anxiety and perceived incompetence may develop. The derived state of anxiety may eventually discourage a child and lead the child to dropping out.

Danish believes that the best challenges generated for youth by sports (and for that matter the greatest rewards) come from within the child. The child learns to compete against him/herself. This position suggests that the most effective form of motivation should come from the personal goals and potentials the child sets. Later in the book, we will discuss this assumption more thoroughly.

The AFA study also emphasizes that the desire to participate in sports declines sharply and steadily between the ages of 10-18. Many parents already have experienced this outcome, but perhaps would have liked to have their child continue in sports throughout their adolescence. The study suggested that less than 21 percent of high school students were involved in even one school sport. It seems that social activities, such as dating and merely "hanging around," become more popular as the children age. Passive activities such as watching TV, also become more frequent.

The study concludes by providing a series of suggestions that communities, parents, and coaches are urged to consider. The AFA highly suggests that communities develop definitions of success that are not solely based on winning and the points on the scoreboard. Many of our own tenets match the statements concluded from this study. We will incorporate these suggestions as well as others in appropriate chapters of the book. However, we would like to summarize a few of the major suggestions. The following represents the critical comments:

• Try to develop a realistic perspective and expectation for a child. As parents and coaches, we need to remember what we were like at the child's age and how capable we were then. We shouldn't judge children on what we can do right now.

• We need to realize that "fun" and skill development are the key elements that children want to gain from sports. We shouldn't deprive them of these aspects, or perhaps they will want to stop playing.

• We all have to develop an understanding of what our own child wants from sports. Not all children want the same thing. You need to talk and listen to the consumer (**the child!**).

• We need to know how to communicate with children, so we can empower them. Furthermore, listening to children allows us to better understand what they want and how they feel about their experiences.

The Road Well Traveled: Sports and Childhood
The Flavorful Journey of Children: Concluding Remarks

The well-traveled road of children and sports leads to many junctions. Unfortunately, we are not mind readers, and we never really know which is the best direction to take at some junction points. We use our intuition and our experience to make solid decisions. Nevertheless, we never truly know which is the best choice. The best choice for one child may not be the best for another. Choices for involvement and the degree of competition differ from one child to another. Sometimes outcomes are influenced by a series of circumstances, or even by fate. These circumstances can either make the journey a more positive or a more negative one. We must try to do the best we can with open and honest efforts.

Parents need to learn to respect their children's individuality. The interactive journey of sports in childhood is potentially rich with vast opportunities. For most children, these experiences will represent some of the greatest highlights of their childhood. For others, the experiences will be contaminated with disappointments, with perceived failures, with a sense of emptiness and discouragement. What we strongly yearn for is that parents will not try to control their children's destiny. Remember, it is the children's game and we are primarily involved as supporters. Children need to know that their parents are behind them and are supporting them.

What we hope to provide you within the following chapters are guidelines that represent a map, of sorts, that will help you understand the value of sports. Although our messages in this chapter are basic, we hope that the inspirations behind them are quite persuasive. Sports, to children, are their way of celebrating youthfulness. It represents constructive opportunities that children can take to expend positive energy and interact with their growing world. The following are some of the highlights incorporated in this chapter:

• Sports activities represent constructive avenues for motor and emotional development.

• As observers, parents must respect their roles as spectators and supporters.

• Sports fill major hours in childhood. The experiences are reflective of some of the major milestones that occur in childhood.

• Children can be responsible for regulating and organizing their games. Parents need to give children opportunities in which they can informally play their games. Unfortunately, with organized sports, adults feel the necessity of getting overinvolved. We think that children need to be taught and should improve over the years. However, this is not the main objective of involvement in sports during childhood. Although to some degree we all would like to see growth in all children, the most important goal needs to be fun. Sports can be a constructive, positive outlet for our children. Adults should not take away from children the spirit within the game.

• The journey throughout sports can explain a cycle of life that begins with being a competitor and may end as an observer and a mentor.

• Children must feel that they have choices before participating.

• Sports involvement can help children learn many lessons

in life. Issues such as confronting success and failure, handling frustrations, being part of a team, and coping with competition are all examples of some of the lessons that can be learned.

• There are three types of children on any team. There is the *athlete* who possesses all the talent; the *competitor*, who is hard working but might be quite self-centered; and the *link*. The children who represent the link are ones who put the team first and will sacrifice their needs for the sake of the team. Although all teams need athletes who are skilled and have the desire to be competitive, they also need to have members who link all the teammates.

• Children must be aware that their attitudes are contagious in sports; those who believe in their competence are better off than those who do not.

• Team building and the importance of being a contributor are ingredients that are modeled in sports.

• We must help our children understand that defeat is only a postponement of a possible victory. Children need to learn that they cannot run away from their problems.

• Parents need to gain an appreciation that the events in their children's early lives will only be memories in the future. Helping them to make this time a rich and rewarding experience is the ultimate goal.

References

American Footwear Association. (1991) *American Youth and Sports Participation.* North Palm Beach, Florida: American Footwear Association.

Dryden, K. and MacGregor, R. *Home Game.* Toronto, Ontario: McClelland Stewart, Inc.

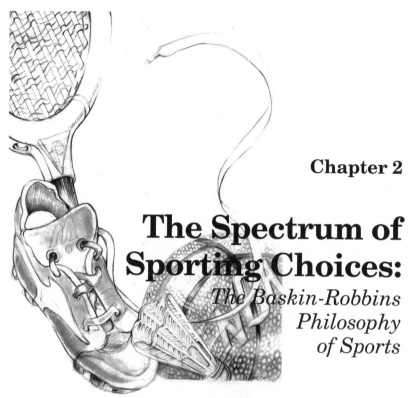

Chapter 2

The Spectrum of Sporting Choices:
The Baskin-Robbins Philosophy of Sports

As children, a memorable event for many of us was a regular trip to an ice cream shop. The anticipation of getting there was only exceeded by having the cone in our hand. The choices were always so simple; the shop only carried three major flavors—vanilla, chocolate, and strawberry. Sometimes the store carried the Neapolitan style, a combination of all three. In spite of the fact that our choices were limited, many of us remember with fondness the joy that came with the first lick. For some younger children it was hard to narrow the choices down to one of the three available flavors.

Similarly, it is hard for parents and other adults to imagine what it must be like for children of today to select a sport because of the broad spectrum of choices. Helping a child select a sport should be an opportunity that we all look forward to. Sporting activities should bring great joy to our children and families. This unearthing of a unique treasure may change the lives of many children and their families. We hope the discovery will be a venture filled with excitement and joy.

The Baskin-Robbins analogy points to the 31 flavors offered in their stores (and dozens more that rotate through their stores from time to time—more than 100 flavors in all!). For some children, it is a challenge to narrow the choices. Not only are the flavors more abundant, but the combinations and methods of presentation are more numerous.

As with the choice of one from a wide array of ice cream flavors, some parents and children are not aware of the tremendous diversity of sports opportunities and the various skill levels that are available to children today. Most people spend a great deal of time studying magazines like *Consumer Reports* and searching for the best prices for major purchases. Few adults, though, take comparable time to shop around and make well-informed choices when it comes to selecting their children's sport activities.

Who is the best person to determine a sports choice for our children? Why should we take second best when, in other areas in our lives, we lead with more assertive and logical choices? In this chapter our major emphasis will be on helping parents to become informed shoppers who recognize the skills required and the level of competition desired. These are decisions which will impact families for a long time.

Overview of the Chapter

This chapter will focus on several subjects. Our major thrust will be to answer many important questions that are often asked by parents who are about to register their children or who have children already involved in organized sports. The major topics are as follows:

1. Understanding the choices available to parents and their children and the stages that parents should consider in helping their children get involved in organized sports.

2. Methods of evaluating which sports and levels of competition are best suited to a particular child.

3. Understanding the concept of being a guest at a child's activities.

4. Questions that parents have with respect to children with distinct needs. The four major categories that we will specifically consider are the superchild, the younger athlete, the gifted athlete, and the challenged athlete.

Starting at the Beginning:
Parental Commitment is a Must!

Although we believe that it is your child's game, we also realize that before a parent registers a child into any given program, the parent should consider his/her commitment. A parent needs to look at the time, energy, motivation, and resources s/he is willing to dedicate to a child's avocation. When a family considers all the variables and the parents truly come to a positive conclusion, they are ready to encourage their child to begin the process. Without strong parental commitment, the zest for active participation may become dampened.

How should parents go about helping their children select a sport? Although the approach may vary slightly, depending on the child's age, the most important element is for the child to have a strong interest and desire to participate. Time may be needed to acquaint the child with the available choices and opportunities. Most children do not know all their alternatives. They need to be presented with a realistic menu of options.

Children are exposed to many sports choices every day. They see their favorite activities on TV, hear about them on the radio, and watch their friends, parents, and other family members play in formal and informal settings. What are children interested in? This is an *obvious question* that needs to be answered. Too often, we take it upon ourselves to make these choices for children, rather than allowing them to choose independently.

The Spectrum of Sporting Choices

The alternatives offered to our children should realistically consider the parents' views. For example, how far and how often is a parent willing to travel to an activity? Are the parents willing to adapt their schedules so that the child can participate? Finally, to what degree will the costs become burdensome to the family? Parents need to make a commitment to the sport activity, in terms of time and resources, in order for the choice to be meaningful. It takes time driving to and from activities, attending practices, games, and possibly tournaments in other regions. Parents must review the financial costs associated with equipment, fees, travel, etc. Other choices may need to be made that consider the parents' commitment capabilities if "Plan A" is not feasible.

When possible, the desires of our children should be the first priority. Children should not be enrolled in an activity just because the activity was a parent's childhood favorite. The child's involvement over the years (positive or negative) could have a major influence upon his or her well-being and quality of life.

Inventorying the Resources Around You

There appears to be a natural progression of steps that needs to occur in helping a child select the most appropriate sports alternatives. As with anything else, you need to start at the beginning, which means getting your child's input. It does not matter how old the child is—s/he must make the first move, or at least concur with the decision.

When a child is not aware of the possibilities, parents should review the wide array of options. We call this *inventorying the opportunities*. In the following section we will discuss the stages of inventorying.

A: The child's interests
B: The child's strengths and assets that relate to successful athletic participation

C: Accessibility of the opportunities

D: Competition versus cooperation—options available in the selected sports; cooperative versus competitive leagues; and levels or degrees of competition

E: Selecting a sport

F: Selecting a sport—financial and other commitments that the family may need to incur (such as driving to the events and how often one is expected to be at events)

A: Your Child's Interests

Children's interests determine their involvement. Parents should survey their children to find out what the children's interests are. Exposure is a wonderful approach. By broadening the child's horizons, new doors may open. This exposure should not only include team sports, but individual activities such as karate, gymnastics, swimming, tennis, and other related activities. Parents should take their children to observe new activities and talk about their impressions. Sometimes children's interests are heightened because their friends are involved. For whatever reason they select an activity, the first step must really be *their* interest in the activity.

B: Assessing the Child's Strengths and Assets

Parents should consider the child's developmental level and assess whether the child will achieve a sense of mastery in the selected activity (or recognize the appropriate level of competition). The motor skills necessary, combined with the level of maturity, are two major factors to consider. Unfortunately, there are children who have great differences in motor abilities and emotional strengths which can cause challenges for children, teammates, and coaches.

For example, six-year-old David is an outstanding soccer player, at least in terms of physical skills. He has a great deal of tenacity, enthusiasm, and drive. However, David cannot handle losing. After each match, his parents cringe at the thought of a loss and having to deal with David. He says nasty things to the other children and he blames them for the defeat. He leaves kicking, screaming, and crying, an outcome that his parents want to avoid. After the game, his parents try to console David, but they find the process exhausting and discouraging. They question their choice for David and wonder what toll this has taken on David and his teammates. However, David's parents do not give up and keep supporting him. They work hard to help David overcome his behavior. David's coach also recognizes that he has challenges and is very committed in helping him. He spends time with David before matches and at difficult moments during games. The coach's attention and recognition of David's behavioral challenges have a positive impact.

The main point, especially with younger children, is that there may be marked differences between a child's motor and emotional development. For children to be successful, coaches and parents must accommodate these differences and be supportive of the child and his teammates.

Then there is Jonathan, who is highly endowed with motor skills but who struggles emotionally. He is constantly being screamed at by his coach because he is not paying attention and is not as involved as he should be. Jonathan has an attention deficit disorder, a behavioral syndrome that impacts about 6% of children in the United States (we will discuss AD/HD in more detail later in this chapter). As a consequence, Jonathan has difficulty sustaining attention. He is impulsive and easily distracted. On the bench, he appears to be fooling around, and on the field he has difficulty staying focused.

Both of these examples illustrate the struggles that may develop when there is an inconsistency between a child's physical and emotional development. Families must become aware of the skills necessary to play at a desired level of competition. For example, a child like David could participate in a soccer program where the competition is minimized. Furthermore, he should be matched with a coach who is experienced with children who have difficulty with losing and is willing to work with him in this area. Over the years, emphasis on this initial foundation will strengthen David's character (although research does not support the idea that participation in sports necessarily enhances character or moral development, many professionals feel that sports participation can really help) and make him a better team player.

C: Accessibility of Activities

Accessibility to sporting venues is one of the greatest barriers that confront families. Sometimes a child's interests cannot be accommodated in the neighboring community, and families have to make a decision about how far they will travel to participate. If the games and practices are too far, or otherwise inconvenient for the parents, families may see a child's participation as a burden.

Some parents develop a circle of support with other parents on the team. This group of parents works with members in transporting children to and from practices and competitions. Parents exchange telephone numbers (and electronic-mail addresses) and develop convenient car pools.

As time goes on, some families become involved with each other and extended families evolve. They often meet and do things as part of a larger group. Many children enjoy this side benefit and usually encourage their parents to get actively involved. Although everyone seems to benefit, sometimes parents are resistant because they do not want their entire lifestyle to be locked into the sport. Other parents may just not feel comfortable in this type of setting or may not be as sociable.

D: Competition versus Cooperation

A few decades ago, many more children were involved in informal play, such as sandlot "pick-up" games. Although the games were competitive, they were less formal and unregulated. Children did not have the adult supervision and structure of organized sports. In most cases, the outcome was extremely positive. Children learned to get along, resolved disputes, included everyone in the game, reaffirmed friendships, and had fun.

Children need the opportunity to celebrate their youthfulness in unstructured activities, and should not be hurried to grow up faster than necessary. The time will come when they will be confronted by the negativity that structured competition sometimes elicits. For this reason some question why children, especially very young ones, are pushed into organized sports so early.

It may help to define competition at this point. Most of us have learned to view competition as a process that compares how we do against someone else, or another team as the case may be. Accordingly, there are winners and losers, based on who does "better" than the other person. One can also compete against nature or the environment (as when you go mountain climbing) or against some standard (trying to run a distance in a certain time). However, our children do not necessarily view competition in the same way we do, although they learn quickly about winners and losers. Rather, we should emphasize the idea that comes from the word *competition* and its Latin roots—*com*, meaning with, and *patere*, meaning to seek. The idea of competition is actually to seek excellence together. This is almost a cooperative model, where together we do our very best with/against each other, and the best on this day wins. However, as we will see in defining success in Chapter 5, we can therefore *both* be successful. This is the real idea of participating in sports—that we are all successful based on our own, individualized orientation.

At what point is a child ready for competition? Is age the only factor or should other factors be considered to make an appropriate decision? Some factors that quickly come to mind that will help a child compete more readily are the child's maturity for his or her age, his or her physical development, and the ability to deal with pressure. This is a question that all parents need to think about, especially with respect to younger children. Parents of older children should be concerned as well with this issue, and should concentrate on the degree or level of competition that a child is capable of handling.

Once children choose a sport they like, attention needs to be given to the level at which they are capable of playing. Additional attention should also be addressed to the degree to which children are willing to sacrifice their other interests for the sake of the sport. Some children want to play, but do not like to practice. Realizing that there are individual differences, parents must ask themselves what is best for their children and the family and investigate what is available.

Different leagues have different emphases. Some leagues stress competition, others participation. You can easily identify competitive leagues by their attention to win-loss records, league standings, playoffs, and crowning champions at the end of the season. These leagues adhere to a professional sports model in which winning is emphasized to the exclusion of all other factors.

Unfortunately, many of society's messages are focused in this direction, particularly in relation to sports. Even though both teams in the Super Bowl (the National Football League's championship game) have won their conference titles and have emerged victorious after a long and difficult season, the Super

Bowl loser is still ultimately seen by society in general as a second-rate team.

Many people have a thirst for victory that is insatiable. Unfortunately, for some children the agony of defeat can definitely be a losing proposition. They are just not emotionally ready to accept a negative outcome. Although this is more common with younger children, it is common in older children as well. Children who face this dilemma need guidance from their teammates, coaches, and parents so they can accept losing matches. Sometimes this can be taught through observing other individuals handling the losses, while in other cases it might involve teaching children positive self-talk, self-monitoring, and behavioral self-control. We must teach children that failure (or for that matter, defeat) is an event, not a person! That concept is difficult for young athletes to grasp, especially when they are encouraged to settle for nothing less than victory.

Parents should not register children in activities in which they will become discouraged. Children become demoralized because the demands or the competitive spirit are too great. At times, discouragement may also occur when a child's perceived quality of performance is deemed unworthy.

Some leagues emphasize a cooperative model. In these leagues there is no emphasis on winning. In some cases, the leagues do not keep scores of the games. Some might ask, "So what do these leagues do?" Generally, they emphasize participation—everyone plays! Each child is guaranteed an opportunity to play, for at least a reasonable amount of time, if not an equal share of the playing time available.

In Little League baseball or T-ball, for example, some leagues have a rule that everyone on the team bats in every inning. The three outs per team per inning rule is swept aside in favor of providing an opportunity for every child to hit (and field). Although many parents (and children) may keep score informally (some parents will continue to act in a competitive style), officially there is no focus on who is winning and who is losing. The focus truly is on maximizing PARTICIPATION. The emphasis is on everyone having a chance to play and each child having fun while doing so.

There are many creative ways in which participation can be maximized. It only takes a willingness to break away from the standard, professional model with structures we are accustomed to, and creatively develop new rules to ensure that participation is maximized. The major benefactors of these creative options are our children, who will find their joy and satisfaction maximized with an increased chance to participate and play.

The key is that parents must decide whether they want their children to play in a league that has competitive values or more of a cooperative focus. Once the family has made this decision, then parents can search for a league, or a level within a league, that meets the desired focus. We strongly encourage parents to ask their children (better yet, let them choose) what type of league they would like to join. After all, it's your child's game!

Within the competitive and cooperative models described, there is a continuum of opportunities, with diversity in expected skills and demands. For example, in the USA Hockey organization, a series of levels is established which determines the skills expected for participation in the sport. Not all children can be expected to play at the highest level. Our suggestions for these rankings of competition are simple. *Be aware of the rankings and select the level that you and your child see as the most appropriate at that time.* League officials may be helpful in providing information on the league and even an evaluation of your child's ability. Over the years, a child's skills will evolve, as the child matures physically and emotionally, and the levels of competition can be changed.

Parents should be aware and understanding of the expectations that come with different levels of participation. If parents have a philosophical difference with the emphasis on competition in a league, or feel their child is not ready for that level of competition, they should consider making other arrangements. The child's age should also be considered in this evaluation. When children enroll in the highest level of competition, parents should anticipate an emphasis on competition. At the fiercest competitive level, it may mean that the coach may not play one child as much as he does others, and this needs to be understood. We believe that this should not be the selected path for a child's first few experiences in a sport. It is very discouraging for children if their expectations (particularly with respect to playing time) differ from the actual outcomes.

Some children interpret membership on a traveling team as conferring elite status. Traveling teams travel outside the immediate geographic area to play teams of comparable skill levels. However, the demands upon team members are considerable and parents should evaluate the child's (and the family's) readiness.

The competitive model must also take into account the child's age. As children become older, there is an unwritten standard that reinforces more of a commitment from a child. Furthermore, the expectations for winning and quality of play are also heightened. When children age, especially in the junior high years and older, it should be expected that more fiercely competitive programs expect the participants to take the games more seriously. Coaches encourage players to be prepared mentally as well as physically for all their games. They expect their players to give the game their all, and to come prepared to reach that goal.

E: Selecting a Sport

There are numerous sports in which one can participate, from individual activities such as swimming, tennis, and karate, to team sports such as baseball/softball, hockey, and soccer. One of the first questions asked should be whether your child prefers an individual or team sport. Are social factors particularly important, such as playing with friends, or having a chance to make new friends? If so, then a team sport may be an excellent choice. A team sport can be ideal in helping children learn to get along with peers. However, if the child likes to participate individually (relying on his/her own talents and efforts), then an individual sport option (e.g., karate, swimming, tennis; all of which are often done in groups with other children, providing some social elements) may be best.

A second question concerns the type of sport. Some sports are better suited for different physical fitness benefits, such as cardiovascular fitness, muscular strength, muscular endurance, and/or flexibility. Sports that are particularly well suited for each of these areas (although this may differ for certain positions, such as goalies versus centers in hockey) are as follows:

BENEFITS

Sport	Cardiovascular Fitness	Muscular Strength	Muscular Endurance	Flexibility
baseball/ softball				xxx
basketball	xxx			
football		xxx	xxx	
gymnastics		xxx	xxx	xxx
hockey	xxx		xxx	
karate		xxx	xxx	xxx
soccer	xxx			
swimming	xxx		xxx	xxx
tennis				xxx
volleyball			xxx	

Those who want to emphasize a particular area of *physical* fitness, or a balance between areas, such as strength and cardiovascular endurance, should consider activities that are strong in that area. The type of sport may also be affected by allergies, asthma, or E.I.A. (exercise induced asthma)—some sports, such as swimming, may be helpful for these.

An additional consideration relates to motor fitness—this type of fitness addresses ability to perform motor skills and includes coordination, balance, speed, agility, and power. Different sports require different levels of each of these areas of motor fitness. Effective coaches will be well versed on the demands of each sport and can help you and your child choose a sport well suited to your child's abilities in each of these areas as well as potential for development.

We have occasionally heard of parents, coaches, and children using steroids to increase size and strength, or drugs such as Lasix to lose weight (for youth league football, which may have weight classifications). We cannot urge you strongly enough (!!) to stay away from steroids or drugs—there are many reasons not to use these substances as adults, but they are certainly not for children. These substances are usually taken to maximize performance, but they may not work for a given child and they do have potential detrimental effects on a child's health. Taking these substances is totally opposed to our philosophical approach presented in this book. Please avoid these substances and actively discourage others from using them if you see any evidence of use or interest!

F: Cost and Other Commitments

A very important factor that all families have to consider is the cost and other commitments when children participate in sports. Some families will find it impossible for their children to play certain sports because of the costs. Sports such as tennis and hockey can cost hundreds of dollars per year, not to mention such activities as figure skating, where the costs can run into thousands of dollars. This is a realistic barrier that must be honestly addressed.

Siblings may have their choices limited because one child is undertaking an expensive sport. Families have to be realistic with the limits of their budget and evaluate how much of their resources they are willing to commit.

Developmental Expectations: What Should Parents Anticipate

There are a few general developmental guidelines that parents should recognize. Appendix 1 (at the end of the book) has been designed to provide you with approximate suggested expectations in various developmental age groups. When children are younger, one should expect league play that is significantly less competitive. The major goal should be for pure enjoyment. Parents should realize that younger children will need to learn to become more accustomed to playing on a team and working with one another. Remember, before children can learn to compete, they have to learn how to cooperate.

In the midst of programs tailored for the younger athlete, one should find coaches who are more nurturing and supportive. One should also expect that these coaches recognize that all children have the right to play. Our goal with younger children should not be to encourage specialization in sports, but rather to expose children to a diversity of options. Finally with the younger athlete, parents should expect a high emphasis on skill development and learning the basics of a game.

As years progress developmentally, one should expect children to take on more responsibility for their game. Their skills will become more refined, demands will become more apparent (both internally as well as externally), and the competitive edge will increase. This is where children will begin to make choices. Some will choose less competitive programs within leagues due to their skill. Other children will continue their skill growth, but their commitment to the sport will become more intense.

There are no specific age guidelines for when these shifts

should occur. Certainly, children at four or five years of age should be in less competitive programs, and children at 14-15 years of age might be in more competitive programs (although there is certainly room for recreational leagues at these ages as well). The child's physical and, especially, emotional maturity, will tell you where the child may be most successful. Children themselves will also tell you, when you ask them, where they want to play. Some may be ambitious and seek out more competitive settings. Others may be quite comfortable with a more recreational, cooperative orientation and this should be encouraged. The key is participation and having fun!

Parents: We are Guests

Parents constantly warn their children that they have to be on their best behavior when visiting their family's friends because they are guests. In most cases, children honor their parents' request, and are conscious of their actions. When they do not, their parents are mortified. How can my child act this way in public?

The concept of being a guest resembles the parents' role when they attend a youth sporting event. We are guests in the children's world of play, and we must respect their needs. In the same way that children are expected to be in control when they are guests, parents are expected to be on their best behavior.

Children do not need to see parents humiliate themselves for the sake of a game. As guests, we should try not to take charge, but rather follow the lead of our hosts. If we want to help, we can ask, but we should be aware of our boundaries. It would be very awkward for some of us to go into another person's kitchen and take over preparing a meal, especially without the host's consent. This concept should also be honored in children's sports.

Children welcome their parents into their sports world. They want to know that their parents are interested and they value their support. Most of the time they want their parents to come and watch and, occasionally, assist. The key ingredient, however, is asking your child's permission.

It may seem awkward, but because you are entering their world, it is only fair to ask what they would like from you. Do not assume that they need or desire your help. Sometimes children feel inhibited by their parents' presence and need some space. Parents need to become more attentive and assess the distance that children need. It does not mean that children love their parents any less, but perhaps they just want and need some independence. We can be guests, and not be in control.

Children need allies. Win or lose, they need to feel supported. One would never tell a host that you hated dinner. Being respectful, one would not say anything unless the host brought it up. Children also deserve this approach to feedback. Many children will let you know when they are ready to talk, and in most cases will also let you know how much they would like to talk about the event. What children do not need are long drives home with constant reminders of what they did wrong rather than what they did right. Our children need role models who demonstrate good character and values. We will address these issues of communication more in Chapter 5.

The Superchild

Do today's parents feel that they must focus on competition, thereby supposedly giving their children an edge for the future? What are the long-term implications of a value structure that promotes development of the *superchild?*

Much has been written in the popular press about the superchild and the activities in which parents enroll the child to give him/her an edge. In the parents' quest to shape a more accomplished child, is the child losing out on some of the sacred moments of early childhood? Are the goals misguided and misdirected? The poet Kahil Gibran described parents as archers and their children as arrows. Although parents must be strong to support the bow, they cannot totally control where the arrow flies. Thus, is it realistic for parents to place an emphasis on rearing the superchild?

Society appears to consider it socially desirable to raise a superchild. This is, in our opinion, misguided. What children really need from their parents is a sense of *acceptance, support, and love.* In the quest to develop this superchild, what values are we teaching? Are we setting up children or families for disappointment and perceived failure when they inevitably lose? These are issues that must be considered as part of the larger picture. Parents must make educated choices. Our actions may be more clearly understood through hindsight, but that understanding after the fact does not rectify misguided actions or choices.

Younger children may not be prepared to accept the consequences of winning or losing. The outcome of competitive games can cause hard feelings in the child, embarrass the parents, and frustrate the coach. Coaches who work with young children have to recognize that their team may react negatively to competition and unrealistic demands. In Chapter 5, we will describe useful feedback that coaches and parents can give.

Probably the greatest concern for the athlete, especially young ones, is overemphasis on preparing a child to be a super-athlete. *Remember*—children should be involved in sports for the long run. We do not want to discourage children so that after a few years they want to give up because the joy in the sport is gone.

Alan is an 11-year-old who has been involved in organized hockey since he was four. He is a good athlete at his age and his parents urged him to participate in a travel club. At first, this was very exciting and rewarding for Alan. He was thrilled with all the attention that being on this elite team brought him. However, with this experience came further expectations, and demands on his time as well as his talent.

Alan became frustrated and disenchanted with the expectations of his parents and their unreasonable demands. At the age of 11, it became a battle to get Alan to play. His parents were often harsh about his performance, and he appeared to avoid conflict with them. He eventually decided to retire from organized sports and be a regular 11-year-old (who would ride his bike and play with the neighborhood kids).

Richard is a 12-year-old elite baseball player. He too has been playing since he was very young. Over the years, his parents felt a strong need to shop for teams and try to find the best place for their son. To them, the best arrangement for their son was more recognition of his talents and more time in the game. Unfortunately, these actions created animosity between Richard and his teammates (throughout the various teams). Consequently, Richard withdrew from active sports without any sense of accomplishment. In retrospect, one wonders where he would be today if the family had just left him alone and positively encouraged his involvement.

To witness a group of athletes who are misdirected can be a sad experience. Coaches who expect children to be adults and make unrealistic commitments are misguided. What do children learn early in their lives when they are told they are not living up to the expectations of others? They are treated harshly for no apparent reason. They are made to feel inadequate and to feel that it is beyond their power to make changes in their lives.

Groups of Children with Special Concerns to Consider

Sports and the Younger Athlete

There are probably more questions than answers when dealing with the young athlete. This is true because there are so many individual differences among children, especially when they are very young. Parents do not want to push children into activities they are not ready for. Some of the most common questions we have heard over the years are:

The Spectrum of Sporting Choices

1. When should children be enrolled in organized sports? Is there a good age?
2. How much should parents expect from a young child?
3. How does one balance skill development, good sportsmanship, and the importance of play?
4. Will enrolling the young child push him or her too quickly?
5. What should be the correct amount of discipline? What should we look for in a coach who deals with this age youngster?
6. How competitive should be the activities be?

So many parents are excited to see their children in uniform that they sometimes lose the point of why they should play. With the vast array of choices available, many parents are confused about the options they have and what to expect.

We strongly believe that one should be cautious in enrolling younger children in organized sports. Experiences for younger children must stress fun. All other benefits should be considered secondary. The social experiences that come with sports participation are crucial. Younger children benefit most from this dimension. Younger children are generally not product-oriented and are more concerned with the process, with the here and now. The action excites them, and they are more interested in playing than they are in the score or in their actual performance. It is almost always the adults who have strong convictions about competition and winning. The desired outcome for most young children is fun and companionship (where the emphasis should be!).

Many variables must be considered. How young is too young? Starting a child younger than five years of age in any league raises questions. We must consider the child's motor skills and emotional readiness. We must make certain that the child is developmentally ready to be on a team. We have seen many children who have enrolled in leagues which are geared to the younger child. League play can be adapted so that young children can learn a little about the sport, sportsmanship, and playing on a team. However, the expectations should be basic.

The primary goal should be a structured fun experience. However, there are always exceptions to the rules. There are youngsters who become very reactive when they lose, or when they are not the main source of attention. These children do not seem to be ready for organized sports. Their parents worry about the child's reactive episodes, and how the negative experiences could influence the future. Our recommendation is for parents to hold off for a little while, until they and the child are ready. Parents can set up informal opportunities, where a child does not have to follow very specific rules. Parents do not want children placed in situations where their behavior might jeopardize team performance.

Attention must be given to the child's developmental level. Is the child emotionally and physically ready for the sport? Are expectations realistic for the child to achieve mastery and success? Just because the uniform fits does not mean the child is ready! Realistic guidelines need to be established so that children can be challenged without losing sight of the true goals of having fun, learning skills, and enjoying the companionship of others.

The Spectrum of Sporting Choices

It is ironic that we expect children to learn to be competitive when some are not even ready to be cooperative. Psychologist Jean Piaget notes that competitive skills come after a child has mastered cooperation. It is amazing to see coaches and parents who expect their children and teams to compete, when the children struggle to work together as a team. Are we expecting too much from young children to play in fiercely competitive activities? Yes! Many leagues for pre-school and younger children do not keep score (even if parents sometimes do informally) and keep the competition to a bare minimum.

The idea of starting young children in competitive sports is based on the premise that these children will have an advantage over other children who learn the sport at a later age. Ironically, research does not support this contention. In fact, some of the studies show adverse outcomes, especially when the child's participation isn't entirely voluntary. For these children, burnout and attrition from the sport often occur. Some parents are persistent and push their children. There are many horror stories of parents who push their children to participate in organized sports. Overtly or covertly, some of these stories indicate that the parents' love and respect for the child is not unconditional. Some parents are so forceful that their love and devotion is contingent on the child's participating and, even worse, succeeding (winning!). This type of contingency is obviously something to be avoided—our love and respect for our children should be unconditional.

What is most exciting about younger athletes is their true love for the activity. They do not seem excessively concerned about the outcome but are involved for the mere joy of playing. Over the years, we have seen excellent opportunities established for younger athletes. The rules are modified and the children's dignity is preserved. Activities are altered so that the lessons of good sportsmanship and persistence are integrated.

There is a seven-year-old who sleeps in his uniform the

evening before his game. He is in love for the first time. He cannot wait for the event to happen. He is excited and delighted. When asked why he plays, he says he loves to be involved on the field and be a member of a team. He also loves the side benefits of team involvement, such as the pizza parties and being with his friends. He dreads the end of every season because the parties and the games come to an end. Parents who recognize that there are many other benefits to sports involvement beyond competition and winning are enlightened and encourage this type of youthful commitment and love. Early experiences in organized athletics must be guided so that all children can have a sense of accomplishment. These experiences are the vital foundation that will support future sport experiences. With proper direction and support, young children will have opportunities that are rich and complete. They will also have a circle of support in the family and friends who watch and support in awe, seeing the spirit of the child express itself through sports. Younger children should also diversify their interests. There is no reason that children should put all their eggs in one basket. Exposure to many different activities is desirable.

Probably one of the greatest mishaps for younger children is what is known as the *hurried child syndrome*. David Elkind (1981) describes a phenomenon which happens to young children when they are pushed to do things that are beyond their years. Adults hurry children when they expect them to feel, think, and act much older than they are. Unfortunately, this also puts great demands and stress on the children to adapt. Elkind explains that some hurried children are so involved in structured activities that they are denied informal play. Having our younger children always registered in formal activities cheats them of developing and initiating their own pursuits.

The following questions may be valuable for parents to think about before registering a young child in organized sports. What are the implications for very young children who receive constant instruction on the sports they play? Is a child in danger of becoming unnecessarily dependent on adults for guidance and support? Is there ample time in the child's schedule for informal play? Should children learn to develop skills serendipitously or, for that matter, more informally when they are young?

Athletes with Special Concerns:
The Gifted and Challenged Athlete

Children bring to the sports arena a variety of talents and skills. Since diversity is expected, there has to be latitude in our options that acknowledges both gifted and challenged athletes. Gifted athletes are those who have in abundance the physical and psychological skills necessary to succeed in sports. Challenged athletes are those who do not appear to have the physical and psychological skills to readily succeed in sports; for them, quality performance is a challenge.

The issues that pertain to children whose skills fall under either of these categories are of greater concern as the children mature. In the first few years of participation, individual differences can be handled more easily. Coaches can make accommodations so that children can thrive with their strengths and limitations. However, as children age, expectations change and some children may want a more competitive program. These children may be better able to handle the pressures that come with competition and possess the skills needed to succeed.

Who can judge whether a child has the skills, physical and emotional, to enroll in more advanced levels? In ideal situations it should be an outsider who does not have a vested interest. Wouldn't it be great if every league had an outside panel that made itself available for evaluations? Panels could be set up so that members did not evaluate children from their local community, so that potential bias could be minimized. Too often, either parents or people too close to the situation make the ultimate decision on participation. Their decisions may be genuinely one-sided and place a child in an uncomfortable dilemma.

An elite athlete, at any age, has to have superior drive in addition to superb skills. Parents should realistically examine the alternatives that are available to make the best educated choice for their child. Before enrolling a child in a more advanced level of a sport, one should consider a series of questions. If a majority of responses are affirmative, a more competitive experience may indeed be appropriate.

1. Would a group of evaluating coaches be in agreement that the child is exceptional in comparison to his/her teammates? If they are not all in agreement, then perhaps the child really is not ready or would not be the best candidate for advancement to a higher level of competition.
2. Does the child have the desire and tenacity to play in an elite program? Is the child mature enough to handle the rigors and pressures associated with this type of program? The excitement of being on a select team wears out over time for some children, and they may feel overwhelmed or trapped by expectations. A competitive figure skater or gymnast, for example, is expected to practice several times a day, for many hours, to be ready for competitions. Is the child ready to accept the rigors of that commitment?
3. Does the child have a temperament which allows competition without being self-destructive?
4. Does the child have high self-esteem to cope with the expected demands of the new level of competitiveness?
5. Is the family willing and able to accept the costs and other responsibilities that come with enrollment in the new level?

Children are often brought into new situations without adequate preparation. Unfortunately, when this happens, children can be negatively affected. Adequate planning can avoid these negative effects, such as:

1. Making sure the child is aware of what the new level of competition entails.
2. Attending some games/events of this league/level to see what the atmosphere is like.
3. Taking some trips similar to the teams (if it is a travel team, for example) to see what the trips involve.
4. Talking with other children and parents to get a feeling for what to expect at this next level of competition.

For some children, being a member of an elite team could be the best thing that could happen to them. Josh comes to mind as one example. Sports are Josh's life. Like many young talented teenagers, he dreams of being a professional athlete one day. Even more importantly, sports involvement has impacted his life. He was not doing well in high school and was not a happy youngster. His only true positive social outlet was playing hockey.

Over the years, people began to recognize Josh's hidden talents and began to challenge him. He became very serious about the sport and, in his free time, practiced and refined his skills. He started to develop a positive way of thinking—a prerequisite to more advanced levels. His attitudes changed and his desire was apparent. Josh truly was prepared for the demands that would be placed upon him. His elevation to a higher level was totally merited.

More often, though, one can think of children who just are not ready and, unfortunately, fail and want to give up. For some families, being a member of a team consisting of the "privileged few" has a social status. Sometimes it is not the child's desire to play for a specific team, but rather the parents' desire.

Many parents are becoming more conscious of how favorable opportunities can be facilitated or rejected due to the circle of individuals one either knows or, perhaps, does not know. We call this phenomenon being aware of the political underground (or political climate) in youth sports. Unfortunately, this political machine does not always function with the best interests of children in mind.

There are families that are willing to gamble and acquiesce to this group. They spend an enormous amount of time trying to meet the correct people, who may be influential for their child in the future. Sometimes parents sacrifice their principles so their child is placed on a team or becomes eligible for future opportunities.

The climate and the conditions that the children are forced to play under can be offensive. Mr. and Mrs. Smith are parents who are very domineering. Over the years, they have invested energies and resources developing key relationships with leaders of the various subgroups in the political underground. They make all the decisions without their son's consultation or consent.

The Smiths constantly enrolled their son in training activities to refine his skills. With all the demands they placed on him, they appeared to have taken the fun out of the sport. Although he enjoys the competition, he is not in love with all the outside commitments. He dreads the ride home after a tough game because his parents figuratively grill him about his performance. They usually do all the talking. He listens and cries. His parents are so concerned about his image that they chastise him when he makes errors. How long will he be able to hold up under this misdirected pressure? This outcome can and must be avoided. The child's best interests must be taken into consideration.

The Athlete with Challenges
The needs of youngsters who are challenged are equally im-

portant. Words do not do justice to the intense feelings that children experience when they are rejected, or made to feel incompetent. What is it like to be a child who rarely gets into a game? What must it be like for a child when it is his/her turn and everyone expects the worst? In the old *Charlie Brown* cartoons, Charlie's teammates expected him to always fail. Did Charlie eventually fall victim to perceived inadequacy? Is this fair for a child? What is important for all adults to realize is that all children learn differently. If we can make concessions and adaptations, all children can play the games and each can develop a sense of pride.

We can view the athlete who is challenged in two major categories. First, there is the child who physically lacks the skills required to succeed. We are talking now more about the child who is awkward or has delays in gross motor development, the clumsy child who has difficulty running, jumping, catching, and throwing, versus a youngster who may have a physical disability due to a birth defect, a genetic condition, or, perhaps, an accident such as a spinal cord injury. Second, there is the child who struggles behaviorally. Negative behavioral symptoms may be due to poor discipline, family difficulties such as differences between family members, a possible divorce, or one of the numerous disruptive childhood conditions such as Attention Deficit Hyperactivity Disorder, Oppositional Deviance Disorder, and Tourette's Syndrome.

Athletes with Behavioral Challenges

Probably the most over-identified childhood behavioral condition is that of Attention Deficit/Hyperactivity Disorder (AD/HD). It is estimated that 6% of children in this country are identified as having AD/HD and are receiving some form of treatment to alleviate its symptoms. An attention deficit disorder is a developmental disability characterized by symptoms of inattentiveness, impulsiveness, and hyperactivity which are considered inappropriate for a child's age or stage of development. The primary symptoms which seem to plague youngsters with this condition can be easily divided into two basic categories.

Children who primarily display the inattentive symptoms of AD/HD are children who fail to give close attention to details and who make numerous careless mistakes. Inattentiveness is exemplified by failure to finish tasks that have been started, being easily distracted, having a short attention span, and having difficulty concentrating on tasks that may appear to be demanding. These children seem to have difficulty sustaining attention and completing everyday tasks. They may appear to have activation difficulties: challenges getting started with something, appearing to be procrastinating or avoiding what they are asked to do. Finally, these children may also have difficulty sustaining their efforts for long periods of time and may appear not to have their minds on the tasks at hand. At times, parents and coaches confuse these symptoms with boredom and laziness and fail to recognize what the symptoms truly represent. We may see these symptoms a lot when children are playing in sports in which they may not be keeping active (e.g., certain positions in baseball and soccer). Children with the inattentive subtype of AD/HD may have difficulty paying attention in their games. They can be easily distracted and, at times, this may be confused with boredom. Coaches also sometimes misinterpret some of these behaviors as a lack of interest rather than lack of vigilance.

On the other hand, children with the hyperactive/impulsive subtype are more likely to appear to have difficulties controlling restlessness. Impulsiveness can be described as acting before thinking, having difficulty taking turns, and constantly shifting from one activity to another. They also may appear to be very active (act as if driven by a motor) and have difficulty remaining still. Children with this subtype of AD/HD may often act impulsively, which suggests being nonreflective and stimulus-bound. For example, "what is on your mind is out of your mouth" is an illustration of what we mean as being nonreflective. A child who is angry at another child may quickly strike out and either say something inappropriate or hit the other youngster. When questioned, s/he may say, "I really didn't mean it." This suggests an inability to self-regulate behavior. Lack of impulse control seems to contribute to a variety of social problems. Impulsive behavior annoys other children, as well as adults, and truly alienates peers.

Unfortunately, all of the previously noted symptoms can cause serious challenges for a child when s/he is in sports. The daily challenges and obstacles presented to the child as a consequence of the characteristics inherent in the syndrome can, at times, prevent the child from fulfilling his or her leisure/sports desires.

More specifically, we can address the issues of social competence and relationships. Many parents and professional leaders would concur that social inadequacies may be the hallmarks of the syndrome of AD/HD. Research has suggested that some of these children act intrusively and boisterously. As a consequence, they may annoy and irritate their peers. Making and keeping friends can also be a challenge and a source of discouragement for children with attention disorders because the core symptoms of inattention, impulsivity, and hyperactivity disrupt interpersonal relationships. Children with AD/HD often experience social rejection. Poor acceptance by peers can cause feelings of isolation, loneliness, and unhealthy self-esteem. The end result can severely dishearten any child.

Attention must be given to these symptoms on the playing

fields to enhance the social abilities of the children. Without proper attention and support, many of these children may fail. Mark Twain once said, "Don't let your son's schooling influence his education." In many ways, he was correct. One's education for life must include an ability to function within the community.

Children with AD/HD can be assisted with various treatment options. For example, some children are prescribed medications such as Ritalin and Cylert which enhance their arousal levels and indirectly influence their inattention and high levels of activity. The medication acts as a tool to potentially impact the behavior. In general, children who have a positive reaction to medication exhibit an increase in on-task behavior, in staying focused, and improvement in social relationships with peers. However, children need to also try to learn strategies for self-regulation and control. Therefore, the beneficial effects of medication usually occur in conjunction with, and at times depend upon, the presence of other interventions that are administered concurrently. We strongly suggest that parents discuss their child's condition with the coach so s/he can integrate the support system established into the child's sport.

We recognize that some families are not comfortable discussing the individual differences of their children. They are reluctant to share with coaches information that would potentially be helpful in working with their child. We suggest that, whenever possible, parents should take the opportunity to educate the child's coach about the child's needs. Not only may it be helpful to your youngster, but to other children whom the coach may encounter in the future.

Finally, children who are being treated with medication may benefit from taking the medication before games. The medication taken could make it easier for the child to concentrate and regulate his/her behavior during a game. Parents should discuss this concern with the child's physician to ascertain if the prescription can be utilized during games. In this way, the child could get the support s/he needs.

Athletes with Physical Disabilities

There are also numerous options that we can also discuss with regard to athletes with physical disabilities. Children with physical disabilities will find themselves in activities ranging from integrated opportunities to specialized competitive or, for some, cooperative levels of wheelchair sports. It is important for the community at large to appreciate that all children thirst for sporting/leisure opportunities, but many reach the fountain in different ways. Therefore, attention needs to be given to the possible accommodations required by children with physical disabilities to participate in their desired leisure/sports choices.

A remarkable accomplishment occurred in 1989, when Mark Wellman, a park ranger, captured national attention by climbing a sheer rock cliff in Yosemite National Park. What made this accomplishment particularly challenging, and hence interesting, was the fact that Mark Wellman was paraplegic. This accomplishment illustrates how anyone can capture dreams. Twenty-five years ago, Wellman's story would not have been reported. In the past, many people would have questioned why it was important for such an event to occur and might have viewed the story in a paternalistic manner. Today, stories of remarkable accomplishments are becoming more commonplace and are being reported as worthwhile endeavors. Numerous worldwide legislative initiatives are helping people become cognizant of the rights and needs of people with disabilities. For example, in the U.S., the 101st Congress passed Public Law 101-336, which is known as the Americans with Disabilities Act of 1990. The purpose of the act is to provide a clear and inclusive national mandate to help end discriminatory acts against people with disabilities.

There are many opportunities and activities for children

and adolescents with physical disabilities. Wheelchair basketball and wheelchair tennis are the two most popular sports for juniors. Only a few modifications are made to the rules of the game in order to keep the game as similar as possible to the non-challenged versions. Quad rugby, road-racing, water and snow skiing, hand-cycling, track and field events, swimming, wheelchair softball, racquetball, and table tennis are a few other available options. *Sports N' Spokes,* a popular magazine dedicated to reporting on the latest developments in wheelchair sports and recreation, includes a section for juniors and acts as a great resource for those interested in further information on featured wheelchair sports.

Some children will need modified or adapted equipment in order to participate in their chosen sports. Activities may have to be modified to assist their participation in the activity, but this does not mean that the child lacks the desire and the capabilities to play. That is one of the most important issues to note!

In the past, schools and community recreation agencies have often segregated activities for children with disabilities. Today's trend prefers to mainstream (to a degree) all children. Adaptive sports are offered as long as equal distribution of abilities are ensured. Such a mixture in activities opens the eyes of all of the participants to see that they are more similar to than they are different from one other (regardless of ability levels). Incorporating integrated activities also breaks down barriers and fosters mutual respect among people.

Finally, as we did in our discussion of the gifted athlete, we must ask ourselves these basic questions as they pertain to all children, including those with behavioral and physical disabilities. Is the child enjoying the experience, and what is necessary for him/her to be successful? Parents should be very cautious to safeguard the emotional integrity of the child and make sure that the situation in which the child is enrolled is indeed the most beneficial.

The Spectrum of Sporting Choices

The keys to successful experiences are *sensitivity* and *reliable adaptations*. Any child should be able to fit in when guidelines are adapted and adjusted to meet the specific needs of the child. The attitude of the coach and the philosophy of the team should be a strong indication of what types of individual accommodations can be expected. Ultimately, the crucial issue is that the child feels a degree of success and is not subjected to negative experiences.

Parents should recognize that, over time, skill levels may improve with practice. No child should be made to feel incompetent when proper guidance is implemented and a support system is in place. Whenever possible, especially for the younger child, provisions need to be implemented so that the child will be successful. Sometimes a child's temper or disrespect can influence how that child is accepted on a team. Unfortunately, it can eventually cause a child to develop a reputation. With proper counsel, a parent can search out a sports option and a sensitive coach that are best suited for the youngster.

Athletes with Cognitive Challenges

We have focused on athletes with behavioral challenges and children with physical disabilities. We will now give some attention to children with cognitive disabilities. We strongly believe that these individuals also have the right and desire to participate in sports. For convenience in understanding we are grouping several developmental disabilities such as varying degrees of mental retardation, autism, and severe learning disabilities. All of these children have some cognitive deficits that may affect their ability to learn and perform daily activities.

Over the past decades, the professional community serving children with mental retardation and other developmental disabilities did not give the appropriate attention to the value of sports and leisure participation. People thought it was foolish to worry about sports for children with these cognitive deficits, when many of the other areas of daily living were such a struggle. Today, the area of leisure and sports is viewed entirely differently. People are beginning to appreciate that there has to be quality in life if people are to lead a satisfying and enriched existence. We believe that a human life is shallow without the joyful experiences which make it meaningful. A complete lifestyle which includes active leisure/sports participation will bring tremendous joy to daily living because one has something to look forward to.

The goal of leisure instruction and sports participation for children with cognitive deficits should be to enhance the quality of life of those children. Sports provide positive opportunities for joy, friendship, and community involvement. Parents should encourage their children to develop interests that can be conducted alone or with others, and activities that involve active participation as well as being a spectator. Although a goal may be to register a child in an organized sports program, parents should also be aware of the value of self-initiated informal play at home. For example, if a child joins a basketball program, s/he can shoot baskets and play at home with the children in the neighborhood or a family member.

In the past, the primary outlet for many of these children was Special Olympics, which was initiated by the Kennedy family specifically for persons with mental retardation. You will be able to find a Special Olympics chapter in your city or state, or you can contact the main headquarters listed in the resources for parents at the end of the book. Special Olympics provides opportunities for children with mental retardation to participate in sport. The program runs year round. Special Olympics also has a program called Unified Sports, which provides opportunities for children with mental retardation and children who do not have a developmental disability to participate in sporting activities together. This is an excellent program that provides integrative opportunities for children with and without mental retardation to play together, learn from each other, and have fun. In communities parents may also be familiar with the Challenger sports program. This program is sponsored by Little League and AYSO, but it primarily provides structured sports options for special populations.

Recreational involvement is a fundamental element to life satisfaction. It is for this reason that we advocate that parents encourage their communities to establish both integrative and specialized activities. Integrative options and activities conducted in the least restrictive environment are now more than ever the accepted direction in the field of developmental disabilities. The position of integrative experiences is also strongly supported in the field of leisure/recreation. Children with cognitive disabilities can participate in sports with other children without disabilities. Parents should be aware of the child's developmental limitations as well as potential prejudice from other children and parents in choosing the best setting for their child. For some, this may mean that the participant will be involved in semi-integrated activities.

To enhance the likelihood of integration, preparation may be needed. For example, the development of a functional Circle of Support makes remarkable sense when assisting children with developmental disabilities in initiating their sports lifestyle. Utilizing leisure coaches, as well as family members, is one example of a potential circle of support. These individuals can help the child get ready for a game, and act as independent coaches to promote successful early experiences. If coaches are taught well, they will eventually create opportunities where the children will fit in more naturally.

Finally, for true integration to become a reality, parents must continue to give attention to improving the likelihood that children with developmental disabilities will have more long lasting and realistic friendships. Efforts need to be made by the coaches and the parents to help the children fit in and to try to develop friendships on and off the sports field. When this occurs, children not only celebrate their joys in the games but outside as well.

As Frank Lloyd Wright suggested, "The longer I live the more beautiful life becomes. If you foolishly ignore beauty, you will find yourself without it. Your life will be impoverished. But if you invest in beauty, it will remain with you all the days of your life." The investment of developing satisfying leisure/sports options for children with cognitive challenges can truly enhance the beauty and satisfaction found in life and make life more meaningful and enjoyable for the children and their families.

Summary

In this chapter, numerous suggestions have been made to enhance the participation of any child in sports. Parents must become informed consumers in order to make good, well-informed choices. One of the nice things about ice cream parlors is that they are there to serve and are willing to help customers make their selections. In youth sports, this kind of service is not available. Great care must be taken by parents and their children in order to select the most enjoyable and supportive options from among the opportunities which are truly abundant.

Only when these tenets are followed will children and their parents be satisfied with their selection. In the ice cream store, a mistake in selection may result in temporary and low-cost disappointment; in sports, an error in selection can have far more lasting effects on the lives of the children who participate.

The Spectrum of Sporting Choices

Key Points

• Gather information to become an informed shopper and take your time to shop for/select the best option, considering the:

    a) child's interests

    b) child's physical and emotional maturity

    c) family situation

    d) league level and type

• Children need the chance to play in both formal and informal sporting activities.

• Recognize that there are numerous choices for a child to play.

• Inventory your resources so you can make the most educated choice.

• Be aware of and understand the expectations that come with a selected level of participation. Recognize the different emphases of various leagues and select the program that most suits the child.

• Be aware of the child's developmental level, both physically and emotionally.

• Try to recognize if your ambitions are misguided, especially with younger athletes.

• Encourage your child so that sport/fitness becomes a life long activity. Remember that children should be involved in sports for the long run. Do not discourage them so they give up prematurely.

• There is more to life than being a super athlete.

• Children bring to the sports arena a variety of skills and talents. There has to be latitude in our options that acknowledges both the gifted and challenged athletes.

References

Elkind, D. (1981). *The Hurried Child*. Reading, Massachusetts: Addison-Wesley Publishing Company.

Chapter 3

Self-Esteem and Sports

"Winners are those people who will do the extra things that losers won't do." — Jack Canfield

This quotation from Jack Canfield stresses that winners recognize that they have to work harder than others to achieve at a higher level. Pat Riley, basketball coach of the Los Angeles Lakers and now the Miami Heat, thinks that excellence is the gradual result of always wanting to do better. This strong belief system represents the values of certain people who do not give up. They do not take for granted their inherited assets and continue to strive to be their best.

In sports as well as activities of daily life, feeling like a winner and believing in oneself are key ingredients to success. A child can be "the best" at an activity, but can be outplayed by children who have a stronger will to win. Who are these individuals? What ingredients do they possess which allow them to achieve at a higher level? Is there a magical formula that transforms children into winners? Are children born with certain traits that enhance the likelihood of healthier self-esteem or can you teach "winning" to make it more likely?

Self-Esteem and Sports

What is self-esteem? A simple way of understanding self-esteem is to recognize how you feel about yourself. When you are accepting of who you are and like and respect yourself, it is assumed that you have healthy self-esteem. On the other hand, when you do not accept yourself and you are often self-degrading, then the opposite may be true, and you may have unhealthy self-esteem. There are many other words that capture similar meanings. Words such as self-concept, self-image, and, for that matter, even self-perception are often used interchangeably.

The California State Task Force to Promote Self-Esteem and Personal Social Responsibility adopted a couple of working definitions. One definition identified self-esteem as *"a social vaccine that may be used to inoculate individuals from life's misfortunes."* Perhaps the key term in this definition is that of a *social vaccine*. When you are vaccinated, it is assumed that you will be protected from something. In this case, it is believed that healthy self-esteem will promote more individuality and assist an individual in promoting and living a more healthy lifestyle. It will hopefully enhance an individual's quality of life and allow him/her to live more fruitfully.

On the other hand, the Task Force also identified self-esteem as *"appreciating my own worth and importance and having the character to be accountable for myself and to act responsibly toward others."* Again, in this definition, we can dissect several important fragments. First of all, the definition recognizes the importance of self-recognition of worth. It really does not matter if everyone else thinks you are great if you do not. You must have this internal recognition and self-appreciation. The last aspect of the definition brings forth a crucial component. It suggests that successful individuals recognize the impact of their behavior and try to be more responsible. Accountability means that you accept the consequences of your actions and recognize how they may impact others.

In the world of sports, children who have healthier self-esteem are more accepting of who they are. In general, they seem more willing to take on personal challenges and do not seem to be so self-destructive. These children seem to have an easier time realistically assessing their assets and limitations. They are more accepting of outcomes and will view them on an individual basis. For example, a child who has one bad game will be able to look at the outcome much more realistically and rebound forward versus a child who is less accepting.

Children bring many assets and limitations to their sporting events. Perhaps one of the greatest contributors to success in sports is the mental health of a child. Healthy self-esteem helps promote risk taking and becoming more responsible for one's actions.

David Brooks (1990), a nationally recognized authority on self-esteem and personal responsibility, suggests that self-esteem is built by a step-by-step progression of successes, and successes are the result of action. He refers to the Four A's as key ingredients for healthier self-esteem. Brooks believes that you must have the right *Attitude* to succeed. Without the right attitude, the process is not ready to begin. From there, the individual must take the steps for proper *Action*, which will lead to achievements. This suggests that there must be a plan to *Attain* success. Finally, for there to be growth, the individual must *Acknowledge* the achievements.

In many ways, this simplified perception of how to maintain healthy self-esteem makes sense. A proper attitude spurs an individual to get something accomplished. This ultimately leads to recognition (either internal or external) and, hopefully, self-acknowledgment.

There are many factors that influence a child's self-esteem. Experiences with one's family from birth to the present date can have an impact on the way a child feels about him/herself. If a child lives in a home that is open and supportive, those experiences will be much more positive than life experiences that are full of anger and ridicule. This area is of crucial importance when we talk about sports. When children are exposed to parents who are always discouraged about their performance, they may want to give up. Often we hear of children who are excited when their parents *do not* attend their games. They say that they do not want them there because they always have negative things to say about their performance.

Similar outcomes can also be found in the child's other important areas of life, such as school, religious and social life, friendship, and sports involvement. In general, no single event or person can determine a child's self-esteem. It develops over time and in many ways is constantly changing because of life experiences. Negative and troubled relationships tend to negate self-esteem while positive social outcomes are potential enhancers.

Children who think positively make it a point to act as their agent. In many ways these are children are their own best friend. They seem to accept their faults and assets and try to take pride in their achievements, both small or large. It is important to realize that this is a developmental process. As children age it is easier to become more self-directed and independent. Younger children appear to be more vulnerable to the opinion and efforts of others. As children age, they can become more empowered to make significant changes on their own. Children with healthy self-esteem in many ways set realistic goals that they can accomplish and try to live a *can-do* lifestyle. This underlying belief system radiates not only within, but also externally. Children learn to respect themselves and try to be their own person, not someone else.

Unhealthy Self-Esteem: Where Does It Lead?

Children who have unhealthy self-esteem appear to have many common harmful characteristics. Stephen Glenn and Jane Nelsen (1987) have identified many characteristics which they believe are damaging outcomes of unhealthy self-esteem.

We have taken the liberty and utilized some of their perceptions as a stepping stone for discussion.

It appears that many of these children have unhealthy self-assessment skills. They do not evaluate well social situations and their personal impact on the outcome. Many children with unhealthy self-esteem also use inadequate judgment skills and do not take advantage of what they learned in the past.

Many children with unhealthy self-esteem struggle in believing in themselves and are not willing to accept responsibility for their choices or outcomes they influence. Some children always seem to blame others for consequences and do not recognize their impact on the result. Finally, children who have unhealthy self-esteem may have weaker perceptions of their value and significance to others. They do not appreciate their capabilities. They often act against themselves and put themselves down. They feel incompetent and in many ways they do not recognize and appreciate their significance and uniqueness.

Children must be nurtured and encouraged. Parents must be aware of the fact that they have a tremendous impact on their growing child. They, along with the child's coaches, must realize that the efforts they spend encouraging and motivating children today, will help children become more reliant individuals in the future.

The Source of Self-Esteem

Healthy self-esteem is a commodity that is in high demand. It is discussed frequently and desired greatly, but it is difficult to acquire. Many individuals genuinely misunderstand the source of self-esteem. They seem to be confused about where it comes from. This is understandable because our society sends mixed messages about it.

One way to understand self-esteem is to distinguish between valid and invalid perceptions. Valid self-esteem comes from the inside-out. It develops and stems from a solid, clear place within us, and it is a variable we *can* control. Although situations in our life alter, our self esteem and our healthy way of coping are the same in all situations.

The difficulty, of course, is that children confuse valid self-esteem with invalid self-esteem. Children may interpret anything that makes them "feel good" as a valid source of self-esteem. That is understandable, because valid and invalid self-esteem can feel similar in some ways. At first, meeting a difficult challenge leaves us "feeling good." Nevertheless, other alternatives that are somewhat antisocial, such as abusing drugs or joining gangs, can also leave us with the same feelings.

One of our primary tasks as parents and coaches is to help our children recognize the difference between valid and invalid self-esteem. If children can do that, they will be better able to make the kind of choices that will provide them with valid self-esteem: the good feeling that comes from a strong, clear place within us, and that will therefore endure. As children grow in their ability to recognize sources of valid self-esteem, they will also learn to approach with caution those situations that let us "feel good," but that come from something outside ourselves and will not endure.

We need not look too far for examples of invalid self-esteem. Our society is loaded with sources of invalid self-esteem. No wonder children are confused. They conclude that the way they "feel good" about themselves is to wear a certain fashion of clothes, to be a member of a gang, to smoke, etc.

How can we recognize valid self-esteem? We can ask ourselves a few simple questions:

- Does it last?
- Can you "take it with you"?
- Does it lead to meaningful relationships with others?
- Does it leave us with a feeling of self-respect and respect for others?

- Can we produce it all by ourselves and without the help of anybody else, or anything else?

It is easy, particularly in our culture, to develop an external base of self-esteem. This kind of self-esteem is invalid. It looks good on the surface, but it does not last. Our culture in many ways specializes in it. Looking good or driving a beautiful car are two examples. Manufacturers in our culture have found ways to associate the possession with their product, like a vehicle, to enhance our self-esteem.

We must be proactive and help children understand the source of valid self-esteem so they do not wander aimlessly to find it. Children must realize that self-esteem is not a commodity that you can gain, lose, and regain. They must realize that self-esteem is a skill that can be learned and practiced.

Perhaps the most significant way we as parents and coaches can genuinely help our children develop self-esteem is to begin the shift in our own lives—away from a self-esteem based on things that happen to us, and towards a self-esteem that comes from a strong, solid place within us.

Success-Driven versus Failure-Avoiding Individuals: How Does This Philosophy Relate to Excellence in Sports?

Every year, many wonder what were the critical ingredients that inspired teams to have winning seasons. So often teams with tremendous talent lose out to teams that have a strong drive to win. In fact, motivation and the desire to achieve are probably two elements that contribute to the overall making of a successful team and its players. It was once said that a person without enthusiasm and motivation is like an automobile without gasoline. The source of energy is depleted and the individual is not ready to engage life.

How an individual is driven and appreciates what causes his/her success and failures is an important dimension for us to understand. Parents and coaches must comprehend what causes children to become more motivated and willing to reach out for success. We will now try to shed some insight into this area.

How does a child understand what causes his/her success or failures in life? Research in the area of motivation emphasizes two major perceptions. One is known as *locus of control* while the other is classified as *attribution theory*. Locus of control represents the study of how one understands what are the causes of success and failures in life. Locus of control relates to an internal belief system that is held by a child that his/her responses will or will not influence the attainment of the desired goal (reinforcement). Some believe that locus of control is somewhat like a generalized expectancy, addressing whether behaviors are perceived as instrumental to goal attainment, regardless of the specific reinforcer. Some children accept the position that external circumstances influence the successes and failures in their life. This outcome occurs when a child perceives his/her actions as irrelevant to the outcome. Acceptance of this position highlights what is known as *external locus of control*. For example, a team that just won a baseball game could attribute their success as being a lark, or, for that matter, they won because the other team was just inadequate. The team does not accept its efforts and skills as a reason for the success. They view the external reasons for the cause of the outcome.

On the other hand, *internal locus of control* looks at the inner factors and their relevance to the outcome. When this position is opted for, a child feels the results obtained were a direct outcome of actions for which he was responsible. In the case of the baseball team, the team would view the win as a result of a team effort, or perhaps the practice they put in. What is important, is that locus of control has a lot to do with understanding what motivates people to be successful. When people believe they do not have any control over outcomes, and the external factors have an impact on their performance, they become victims of helplessness.

The logic of external and internal locus of control can be understood specifically in life activities. For example, a child may feel very competent and in control in certain parts of his/her life but not in others. For instance, a child may be an excellent student, and in the area of academics recognizes how his/her effort affects performance, but in sports s/he externalizes the outcomes. The research on locus of control also points out very clearly that people with unhealthy self-esteem and learning challenges have a greater sense of external locus of control. That means that these individuals do not recognize how they have an impact on their performance or opportunities. They are victims of external consequences.

Attribution refers to inferences made by an individual concerning the causes of behaviors or events. It should be understood that success or failure can be attributed to one of four causal factors: (1) ability, (2) effort, (3) task, and (4) luck. It should be understood that there are a number of causes that are used to explain success or failure in a sports-related context. History in an event as well as comments from others may influence the outcome. The theory of attribution provides an explanation why children participate in certain activities. The theory infers that the children appear to select options that they feel competent in and in which they are more capable of displaying mastery. It seems that the older the children, the more guarded they become. Furthermore, children who have healthier self-esteem appear to be willing to gamble more, and risk being not as successful.

Self-Esteem and Sports

Successful people should view their performance as a direct consequence of their impact on the outcomes. We have to help children develop their sense of competence. They must learn that to be the best, they have to take command of their behavior. Although fate and luck can always affect any situation, children must realize that *practice, positive attitudes, perseverance, and self-determination* are also features that impact their outcomes.

It is equally important to understand that there are children who are success-driven versus others who are failure-avoiding. In both cases, the children may achieve their goals, but get there in substantially different ways. Children who are success-driven are willing to risk failure to become more successful. They seem to appreciate that one can not grow unless they gamble with failure. They also seem to understand that failure is only an event; it is part of a process that eventually may lead to better things.

Where would we be today without dreamers and leaders such as the Wright Brothers, who believed that people could fly, or people such as Walt Disney or Thomas Edison. These are individuals who dared to take chances to open their horizons. Kennedy once argued for what reasons do some people see things and wonder why, while others dream things and question why. Dreamers are risk takers who are challenged to make impact. The world needs people who have the courage to continue without regard to experiencing failure. We must attempt to energize children so they become empowered to reach for their dreams. Empowering children means helping them develop self-respect as well as dignity in their actions. These efforts will enable them to affirm their dreams. As parents, we must be cautious to not discourage our children by telling them that their desires are impossible to reach. They must be more willing to reach out and challenge themselves. Parents and coaches should take to heart this premise, especially when working with young children. We should try to enhance their horizons rather than limit them.

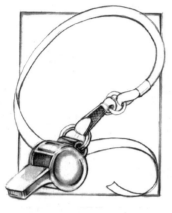

Parents should encourage their children to dare to risk. As we have already noted, without risk taking, children will not be able to reach for their stars. An unknown author elegantly captures the true meaning of risk taking in a short composition. The following represents the final few lines of the passage: *"To believe is to risk failure. Risks must be taken, because the greatest hazard in life is to risk nothing. The people who risk nothing, do nothing, have nothing, are nothing. They may avoid suffering and sorrow, but they cannot learn, feel change, grow, love and live. Chained by their attitudes, they are slaves; they have forfeited their freedom. Only a person who risks is free."*

In many ways, children have the ability to dream because they do not place limits on their ambitions and, thus, weigh down their dreams. Unfortunately, as they get older, they become more grounded and are told to become more realistic.

Some children fear so much that they will not be successful that they avoid opportunities where they may be challenged and risk failure. These children avoid situations so that they can escape failures. What they do not seem to appreciate is the fact that when you avoid failure, you are also inadvertently limiting your opportunities. Your lifestyle becomes more restrictive because you avoid options. A child who is failure-avoiding may withdraw from a baseball team because s/he feels s/he will not perform well. That attitude is self-destructive and causes the child much grief in the long run. The child will miss out on many opportunities, because of this underlying fear. We must help children relax and appreciate their life opportunities. We must also help them clarify in their minds that if they limit their options because of fear, they shrink their chances of securing happiness.

Self-Esteem and Sports

So many of life's fortunes can be obtained through serendipity—discovering things accidentally. The idea of serendipity involves the discovery or awareness of desirable things not sought for. The term was derived from a Persian fairy tale about the three rulers of the Isle of Serendip (Ceylon) who repeatedly travel to the mainland to complete specific tasks. During their travels they never complete their missions, but they always have other valuable discoveries or experiences. Hence, the term serendipity infers unplanned positive discoveries. When people are restrictive, they possibly will lose out on opportunities of which they were not even aware. A tragedy that is hard to explain in words, but easy to recognize in the eyes of wounded child. Many have written about the tragedies of childhood. We have adapted a quotation by Langston Hughes to make it more applicable to children. He suggests "children must hold on to their dreams and ambitions. For if their dreams and ambitions die, then life is like a broken winged bird that cannot fly."

Beliefs that Help Children Lead More Effective and Healthy Lives

We believe that a major contributor to healthy functioning is a set of beliefs that children should acquire. As parents and coaches, we need to be aware of our impact in molding these beliefs. We should also be aware that involvement in all life activities, including sports, tremendously relates to how children master these specific beliefs.

Anderson (1981) identifies numerous beliefs that we will use as a foundation to this discussion. Several of the specific beliefs have been modified to some degree to be more directly related to our discussion.

Belief 1: It is O.K. to make mistakes.

Making mistakes is something we all do. Children who accept this position recognize that they are worthwhile individuals in spite of making errors. These are individuals who recognize that it is inevitable to make errors and they can cope with this. Children must realize that failure is an event not a person. It is realistic to assume that a child will fail many times in life. As Robert Kennedy so elegantly stated, " Only those who dare to fail can ever achieve greatly."

Belief 2: I am responsible for my day.

Many children aspire to learn that they control their destiny. They must learn that they are responsible for how they feel and, for that matter, what they do!

Belief 3: I can handle things when they go wrong.

Children need to relax and recognize they cannot deliberately control all outcomes. They need to accept the position that things usually go fine, and when they do not, they can handle it. Wouldn't this be an excellent belief for people of all ages to follow?

This idea makes tremendous sense in the sports world. Often teams and their players get down on themselves when things do not work out. In fact, their negativity offsets their performance. Children need to recognize that they can handle things when they are not working out. They have to implement a plan that will help them offset their deficits. They need to recognize that they may not be able to change the past, but they still have the power to influence the future.

Belief 4: It is important to try.

This belief is strongly related to the major theme of this book. Children must be ready for the challenges of daily living. Even though they may be confronted with difficult tasks, they must believe that it is better to try than avoid them (as pointed out when we discussed failure-avoiding individuals). Things worth having are worthy of the effort. Children must be challenged to accept this point of view. For some, the challenge will be easier than for others. However, this is a direct goal that we all should have for our children in their everyday activities. Not only will we have to encourage children to live up to this expectation, but we will also have to teach them how to self-monitor and judge.

Belief 5: I am capable.

One needs to genuinely develop a sense of self-respect. A child who recognizes a positive sense of self is a child who will be willing to take chances. Children need to also realize that they should not compare their strengths with anyone else. We recognize that this is difficult, but self-comparison is probably more constructive, at least initially. For example, a child could compare his/her performance to previous outings. As time goes on, external comparisons can also be made. All a child needs to think is: "I am capable and productive." Productivity between children may differ, but believing in capabilities will not. Children need to try to seek the positive in every situation instead of bemoaning what they lack.

Belief 6: I can change.

Children need to know that they have the capabilities of changing their behaviors. Every day is a new experience, and children need to realize they can have an impact on their destiny. For example, a child who has difficulty hitting the ball in baseball must accept the challenge that he could affect his performance with practice. Children have to realize they can enhance their abilities with effort. Unfortunately, some children use negative thinking, which predetermines their behaviors. When children empower themselves to believe they have an impact, surprising outcomes may occur.

Belief 7: Other people are capable.

Children need to respect the individual differences among

themselves. They have to recognize the differences in strengths and limitations among their friends and teammates. It is important for children to begin to recognize that they can assist their peers in achieving their goals, but they cannot solve everything for them. More specifically applied to sports, you can help support a teammate and try to motivate him or her. Ultimately, it will be that child who will have to open up the door and make the change.

Teaching Children Positive Self-Talk

It is amazing how words can impact performance. Too often, attention is solely given to how the child is spoken to and how that may or may not impact his/her self-esteem. It is commonly accepted that criticism and negative comments from others can be very deprecating and damaging. Recently, attention has also been given to the internal language which children use which could be productive or, for that matter, contaminating. We call this private-talk or self-talk. Some in the psychological community strongly believe that self-talk is the most powerful force humans have for self-transformation. Negative self-talk may lead to self-doubt. Ted Turner once said that, "If you think you are a second-class citizen, then you are." It is normal to have some self-doubt, but tremendous self-doubt can be very shattering. It is when self-doubt dominates our thinking process that we eventually develop a failure mode. It is ironic that to eliminate negative self-talk, you first have to be aware that you are using it. We have to teach children that if they always say they cannot, they probably will be right in the end.

Generally speaking, when people tell themselves that an event is beyond their control or they have doubt in their performance, the outcome deteriorates.

A tremendous example that illustrates the power of this strategy is called Kinesiology (discovered thousands of years ago by the Ancient Chinese). This simulated activity involves two individuals. The trainer asks the other individual to hold out his/her arm horizontally and to resist pressure being put on their wrist to lower the arm. After that trial is completed, the individual is asked to repeat the same process two other times, the first time resisting while saying in a low voice something self-incriminating for five seconds, (e.g., "I'm a horrible person or a lousy player") while in the later occasion saying something very positive or uplifting (i.e., "I am an important person or a great person") for five seconds.

The outcome is quite revealing. People quickly see that when they repeat positive affirmations to themselves, they become stronger. They begin to also see how negative self-talk can deteriorate performance. It is amazing to watch an individual realize that when negative thoughts are perceived, performance declines.

Patterns for handling every day disturbing situations are formed in early childhood. One of the most important factors in health is one's attitude. Ironically, self-talk is one of the crucial determinants of attitude. The question that comes immediately to mind is—how do we introduce and teach children the value and impact of self-talk? One of the best ways we have discovered to help a child learn the value of self-talk is to allow the child to observe the value and the effects on the parent or the coach. This form of modeling followed with periodic explanations could help the child see the built-in benefits. We must take it upon ourselves to help children identify their internal voices and help them develop language that is positive, encouraging, nurturing, and realistic.

Additionally we should help children focus on positive self-talk rather than negative, destructive self-talk. Positive affirmations are one of the most powerful procedures we can use to change our thinking and our reactions. Affirmations can become goal-oriented.

Positive self-talk is now recognized as a vital resource for enhancing athletic performance as well as decreasing pre-performance anxiety. Even young elementary-age children are capable of using self-talk and other related techniques to improve their abilities.

Children need to be aware of what they are saying to themselves. If a child continues to pressure himself to *not* strike out, the child may admonish himself and actually keep himself from playing better.

Unhealthy self-talk will ultimately make us feel miserable if we let it. Anderson (1981) points out that there are several kinds of irrational self-talk. The demanding irrational belief suggests the idea that the world should be a certain way. For example, I cannot make a mistake or people *have* to be nice to me. Demands are beliefs parading around facts that are not real. If, for example, we demand that we must not make a mistake, we are going to get very upset because eventually it will happen.

The second type of irrational self-talk is known as *overgeneralization*. This process occurs when we take a little bit of information and blow it out of context. For example, when people believe the negative happens all the time. They believe they are never going to win because we are too inferior.

And, the last of the three types of irrational self-talk we want to point out is the process of *catastrophizing*. Call it the "End of the World" self-talk. When something uncomfortable or undesirable or unplanned happens, a person acts as if his/her entire world has or will be falling apart as a result.

The Magic Ingredients for Healthy Self-Esteem

A question frequently asked by many parents is: what can I do to help my child's self-esteem? Is there any magic formula? Unfortunately, the answer is not simple. As can be seen throughout this chapter, self-esteem is affected in many ways. If we were to select three broad dimensions that we believe impact a child's overall sense of competency, they would be helping children recognize they belong, helping them appreciate their competency, and helping them recognize that they are worthwhile. Although easy to explain and write about, these are three very tough dimensions.

Belonging is of utmost importance. Children need to know they fit in. When this occurs, they feel more comfortable because they realize they are accepted. Probably one of the saddest experiences to watch on a playground is a child wandering around aimlessly trying to find a friend. What compounds this problem even more so is that children need to be accepted into the group to which they want to belong. If a child has a desire to be accepted by one group, but is only accepted by another, the child will walk away feeling empty.

Acceptance and belonging to a specific group is important. Team sports can offer children this option. As discussed in Chapter 1, a sense of belonging is something that sports can easily provide. Being part of a team can be a great motivator. Children definitely begin to see more value in life when they feel a part of something.

A sense of competency is the recognition that one is capable and has something to offer. When children discover their talents and are appreciative of them, they will grow even further. Their sense of feeling worthwhile comes from the recognition they receive from others who indirectly applaud them for their accomplishments. Children need to also pat themselves on their backs for challenges that they feel they have mastered.

Children need to develop a belief system that affirms their convictions. Sometime in their life they will learn to take a stance and note that "I am a capable person who can change if I choose." Children need to appreciate that they can assist in their predestination. Furthermore, children must acknowledge that their life is significant and that they are important. We have to help children unearth their talents so that they can begin to appreciate them. Even a diamond in the rough is not beautiful until it is polished. Children have to realize that at times it may take some effort to get where they need to go. But they must have confidence in themselves—*Faith, that they will prevail.* Finally, children must discover their hidden talents and blossom with them.

Summary and Conclusions
Promoting Self-Esteem in Sports: Guidelines for Parents

Now that we have provided a clear summary of self-esteem, we would like to give you our suggestions of how to promote your child's self-esteem in sports. A majority of these issues have been explained in more detail in specific aspects of the chapter. However, we have altered the issue somewhat and made it more applicable to sports. We hope you will take heed of these comments and realize how important they are in helping your child have success in sporting activities.

When you are accepting of who you are and like and respect yourself, it is assumed that you have healthy self-esteem. Parents should realize that it is of utmost importance that they are encouraging to their child. They have to help their child discover their inner talents and become more grounded. Children who are accepting of their skills are more willing to try to change. They do not walk around feeling discouraged because they have not lived up to their own and others' expectations.

If a child lives in a home that is open and supportive, those experiences will be much more positive than life experiences that are full of anger and ridicule. This area is of crucial importance when we talk about sports. When children are exposed to parents who are always discouraged about their performance, they may want to give up. Criticism and negative comments from others can be very deprecating and damaging. Too often parents personalize their child's performance. They need to realize that it is their child's game. Additionally, they must recognize that, first and foremost, sports should be played for the recreational value of play. Their continued rejection and unpleasant comments will eventually convince a child that the activity is not worthwhile. Learning how to give feedback effectively (incorporating negative and positive elements) is a strategy parents will find valuable.

Parents and coaches must understand what causes children to become more motivated and willing to reach out for success. Over the years, parents should try to analyze what motivates their child to drive for success. When they are more understanding of this dimension, they may be able to apply (or, for that matter, discontinue) approaches which will assist their child in becoming more emotionally energized.

Children must realize that practice, positive attitudes, perseverance, and self-determination are also features that affect their outcomes. Parents must preach and practice these tenets. Of primary concern here is to try to establish an atmosphere where children can celebrate positively their sporting lifestyle. However, for excellence to develop, children have to be guided in realizing that they cannot give up and that they are responsible in altering the outcomes.

We must attempt to energize children so they become empowered to reach for their dreams. Empowering children means helping them develop self-respect as well as dignity from their actions. These efforts will enable them to affirm their dreams. As parents we must be cautious and not discourage our children and tell them that their desires are impossible to reach.

They must be more willing to reach out and challenge themselves. Parents and coaches should take to heart this premise, especially when working with young children. Remember we should try to *enhance* their horizons rather than limit them.

Children must realize that failure is an event not a person. Within sports, this area is always in contention. When children lose important matches, they have to be accepting of the outcome. At all ages, losing is hard to accept. We must make it our goal to help children at a very young age to accept the challenges of competitive sports. Exposure will help children recognize that winning and losing are direct outcomes of any game. The agony of defeat can be devastating. Pictures can be conjured up in our minds of close games in Little League or soccer, where the outcome is very sad. However, as parents we have to help children respect the realities of any game and recognize that any failure should not be personalized. It is merely an event that they have to respect. Children can take lessons of failure and turn them into challenges for the future. What is important for parents to recognize is that it is realistic to assume that a child will fail many times in life. Efforts have to be initiated to help children cope with this dimension of the game.

Things worth having are deserving of the effort. Parents have to help children appreciate that it takes some effort to attain achievement. Tenacity and hard work are two principles that have to be modeled and taught to our charges. Eventually, children who are more driven will take these principles more to heart. Ultimately, they will have to develop more realistic reliance in themselves—*Faith, that they will prevail*. This eventually will help children discover that they have hidden talents that will blossom if the appropriate attention is given.

Children need to realize that it is counterproductive to constantly compare their abilities to anyone else. For children to be successful, they have to be realistic about their own abilities. Children need to know that they have the capabilities of changing their behaviors. They must accept the challenge that they could affect their performance with practice and hard work. Nevertheless, it is detrimental to constantly compare one's performance to that of another. Parents should encourage their children to evaluate their skills, and continue to challenge themselves, using their initial proficiency as a starting point for comparison. Internal challenges can be more productive and realistic. When progress has been made, children can change their focus and begin to externally compare. However, children must begin to appreciate to be the best, you have to start at being *your best.* It is not wise to try to live up to the skill level of others and either believe that progress has been made (but it genuinely has not) or to feel defeated because the standards used were not realistic. As Henry Thoreau suggests, "If a man does not keep pace with his companions, perhaps it is because he hears a different drummer. Let him step to the music he hears, however measured or far away."

When children empower themselves to believe, they have an impact. Again, we return to this crucial premise. The old Zen proverb "when the mind is ready, the teacher comes" really makes extraordinary sense. Children have to be ready and willing to enable themselves, in all aspects of their live, including sports. When this does occur, surprising outcomes may happen.

As parents, we have to teach children that if they always say they cannot, they probably in the end will be right. Negative thinking deteriorates performance on and off the field. Parents must become more conscious of their child's attitude and help model more appropriate alternatives. The major point being, that as parents we should be aware of children's internal thinking and help as much as possible to alter its origin if it is highly negative. *Cannot* usually stands for not wanting or preferring not to, rather than not being able to.

Parents, should help children focus on positive self-talk rather than negative, destructive self-talk. Finally, to continue with what was noted in the previous suggestion, positive affirmations are one of the most powerful procedures we can utilize to change our thinking and our reactions. Children with healthy self-esteem recognize the shattering effects of negative thinking. These children will try to apply positive procedures which enhance their performance, or, for that matter, the outcome.

References

Anderson, J. (1981). *Thinking, Changing, Rearranging.* Eugene, Oregon: Timberline Press.

Brooks, D. and Dalby, R. (1990). *The Self-Esteem Repair and Maintenance Manual.* Newport Beach, California: Kincaid House Publishing.

Glenn, S. and Nelsen, J. (1987). *Raising Self-Reliant Children in a Self-Indulgent World.* Rocklin, California: Prima Publishing.

Chapter 4

Success

Success is what this book is about—*A Parent's Guide to Success in Children's Sports*. However, as you've seen so far, this book is not designed to teach you how to help your child catch a baseball or swim faster or shoot a hockey puck more accurately. Rather, we want you to explore how you define success! We want to look at success for you and for your child, because the two are related. Does success mean winning a tennis match or baseball game? Does success mean closing a deal and getting the deal you want? Does success mean having set your goals and achieved them? Does success mean having tried your hardest, whether you achieved your goals or not? Success can obviously mean many things, and does mean different things to different people.

In our society we often view success within a competitive framework: "I am successful and you are not." Our competitive society prides itself on anointing winners as "good" and losers as "bad." Winners are placed on a pedestal as examples of all that is good; losers are often seen as not worthy of our attention or sympathy. One of the hosts of a local radio sports program sometimes calls some people "Losers," one of the more signifi-cant insults he can give.

The above generalizations about winning and losing are hopefully not characteristic of you or your friends. But many out there do buy into the competitive model as a way of life. "Only the strongest survive." "Survival of the fittest." "To the victors belong the spoils." We don't buy into this model. If you are alone in the jungle, face to face with a tiger who wants you for his next meal, then, yes, it would be a good idea to "win" that encounter. Otherwise, there are alternatives—we can achieve success and excellence through a different approach.

This different approach could be termed a cooperative model. Together, you and I cooperate to achieve the best that we can. In a tennis match or baseball game we both play as well as we can, and the "winner" is simply the one who scores more points or runs that day. It doesn't mean I'm "better" than you, just that I played better today. In closing a deal it means that both of us walk away satisfied with what we've gotten. It means having worked as hard as I could, and hopefully having achieved my goals, but if not, there's always tomorrow.

The cooperative model suggests that we need not defeat or demean someone (as so often happens) in order to be successful. Success becomes something you take ownership of and becomes personally meaningful. Take the case of a game where you played poorly but still won—did you call that a successful day? You won, didn't you?! Yes, but you didn't play well. Similarly, we've all had days when we played superbly and still lost. Was that an unsuccessful day? Yes, if we base the day on winning or losing; but no, if we focus on how we did and what we achieved in terms of quality of play and quality of experience.

Let's look at success more closely. We can consider looking at success in three ways:

1. Success means Winning!

2. Success means having put out 100% effort and done the best you could on a given day!
3. Success means having achieved your potential!

Let's look at each of these perspectives carefully:

1. Success means Winning!

As we noted above, winning is the way society has taught many of us to view success. The socialization process that we are all a part of from our youngest years tells us that winning is good and losing is bad. Winners are respected, honored, idolized. Losers are looked down upon as not worthy of our consideration. Vince Lombardi's alleged quote (he supposedly never really said it), that "Winning isn't everything, it's the only thing," typifies how we often look at winning. Winners are heroes. Anything less (losers) is not valued.

But is this reasonable? There are many more losers than winners. Each game has a winner and a loser (forgetting about ties for the moment). Each season has many losing teams and only one winner. The National Football League is an excellent example of this. The teams play to win the Super Bowl and, if they don't achieve this goal, many teams, and their fans, consider it a losing season. However, making the playoffs is an accomplishment in its own right, and making it through the playoffs to win one's conference and then play in the Super Bowl should be considered successful. Winning the Super Bowl is certainly the ultimate goal, but a team that loses in the Super Bowl, even though it didn't win the grand prize, should still be considered a winning team overall.

Each tournament has many players who don't make it to the victory stand. A tennis tournament with 64 players has many matches, and many winners and losers, but only one eventual winner. An ice hockey tournament with 16 teams features many games, and many winners and losers, but only one eventual winner. Are all the others to be considered "losers"?

Technically, yes, the others have lost matches or games, but do they deserve the negative connotations that accompany the word "loser"? Perhaps the loser actually played very well, even better than thought possible, but lost because the opponent was simply that much better (or, occasionally, because of equipment failure, official's calls, etc.). If this happened to you, would you want the label of "loser" hanging around your neck?

Before you get the impression that we are down on winning, we want to emphasize that winning is fine, but needs to be kept in perspective. We much prefer the way Lombardi's quote has been turned (by noted sport psychologist Rainer Martens) as follows: "Winning isn't everything, but trying to is!" Jimmy, for example, was a good tennis player, and met the number one seed, Joe, in the round of 16 in a recent tennis tournament. Jimmy played very well, and tried his hardest to win, but still lost, 6-4, 7-5. Some might call this a moral victory, because Joe could/should have won 6-1, 6-1 (he was that much better), but Jimmy did his best and, in a sense, won because he tried/did his best.

There's nothing wrong with winning! Trying to win is laudatory, indeed desirable. It means trying your best. But does that mean if you don't win, you're a loser? NO! It means that today, for whatever reason, that W wasn't written next to your name. But you can learn from your experiences and try again. Jimmy, for example, learned a great deal from playing against a stronger, more skillful opponent, and how to use his (Jimmy's) strengths (consistency, returning shots from the baseline) to advantage the next time he played a match. The closeness of the match against Joe, even though he didn't win, also provided a boost to Jimmy's self-confidence, that he could compete with the "big boys" and play better, and perhaps win, in the future.

Just as we're sure you don't like being labeled a loser, you certainly must realize that your child doesn't like it either. One hopeful sign is the lack of emphasis that children place on winning. Winning is way down on the list of reasons for participating in school sports, for example—8th for boys and 12th for girls in one study of 3,900 7th-12th graders. What is number one?—TO HAVE FUN!

We don't believe in the first definition of success! Winning is nice, but it is NOT everything—success means so much more! We do believe in the second definition, which derives from the idea of trying to win. Success is a process, not a product. Success does not equal winning. But the process of doing one's best, as we discuss next, is the key to success.

2. Success means having put out 100% effort and done the best you could on a given day!

What more can one ask of any of us than trying our best or putting out 100% effort? Those of you who like your players to put out 110% effort can ask that. Society uses that expression often, but realistically we can only put out 100%. Doing your best or trying your best is the most important statement you/ your child can make about the importance of an activity and the meaning it has for you.

We would consider you/your child successful if you put out 100% effort—you did the best you could on a given day. That means having tried as hard as you could—having played as well as you were capable. That may mean having won, but often not. The determining criterion of success here is whether you did as well as you were capable of today.

An important point to keep in mind, though, is that we do not always know what 100% is. Sometimes we surprise ourselves with what we're capable of, and that's where the 110% comes into play. With experience comes greater self-knowledge/ self-awareness—we learn over time what it is means to do our best, to put out 100%. This is something that we can assess after a given event, not only thinking back on how we did, but what we did to prepare, how the event went, and what we put into it. You can review this with your child as well—talking about and reliving a match, the learning experiences to take away from the event, and an analysis of not only how one played but how much you/your child put into it. This will help in determining whether you/your child have given 100% today.

3. Success means having achieved your potential!

This third definition is related to the second one. If you like this definition, and consider it in the context of what your child is capable of today, then that is fine. If the context is what your child is capable of eventually (or perhaps remembering one of your child's past, superior performances), then this would *not* be the best definition to use. Potential is, in some ways, a nasty word. Potential is all about what we are capable of achieving. What is the best we are capable of achieving in school, at work, in sport?

In many ways, we can never really know our potential. How can we *really* know what we are ever capable of achieving? Too often we put ceilings on our potential, and never come close to realizing what we are capable of becoming. Our potential is such a complex mix of our genetic capabilities, our physical skills, and our psychological makeup, especially motivation, that determining potential is not even close to being an exact science. In some sports, such as baseball, it is especially difficult to predict, for example, who will successfully move from the minor leagues to the Big Show, the major league level. With all of their experience and knowledge, scouts still often miss future big leaguers and prove wrong with "can't miss" prospects.

Many coaches still try to determine the potential of children with whom they work, to see who will be likely stars of the future. To be a star or champion takes hard work, motivation, support from family and friends, and athletic skills. Most of these skills can be learned. Some athletic "gifts" are inherited. An old saying is that if you want to be an Olympic champion, you must choose your parents wisely! Genes are important in determining what we bring to the sport context. For almost all of us, though, the other factors of hard work and motivation and good coaching to develop skills can outweigh "deficits" in your child's physical makeup. Especially in youth sport, it is a mistake to label a child as one who will never make it. This child might not become a professional athlete, but the child may get a tremendous amount out of participation—having fun, learning skills, and making friends that will provide a successful (!) experience.

If your child's sole goal is to be an Olympic champion or a professional athlete, then your child may be disappointed. Only a very small percentage of children make it to Olympic and professional levels—millions more have dreams of doing so but fall short of fulfilling these dreams. This book is not oriented towards parents and children with the Olympics or a professional career as their goal. Rather, we hope that you/your child's goals are to have fun, learn skills, enjoy being with friends, and get some exercise/physical activity. Your child's memories of playing sports and having fun are ones that will provide a lifetime of pleasure. We have fond memories of our sports experiences as children, ones we carry fondly to this day. Trophies and medals get rusty, and very few of us make it to the Olympics or become professional athletes. But the joys of participating in sport can give us physical and psychological benefits that make each day special and can last a lifetime.

Your Behavior

How does all this translate into your behavior? If you buy into definition number one, that success equals winning, then the only question you need to ask is: "Did you win today?" Does that sound familiar? Millions of parents ask that question after a game or match. Wrong question!! Does it really matter who won? Do billions of people around the world care if your child won a Little League game or tennis match today? NO!

More importantly, your child probably doesn't place that much emphasis on winning either, unless your child gets the message from you that winning is important. Even worse, some children get the message that their parents' love is contingent on their participating and, hopefully, winning. We hear many stories of children who continue in youth sports because they know that's what their parents want, not what they want. Yet the children are afraid of dropping out or changing sports because they're afraid that their parents will love them less if they drop out.

What questions *should* we ask? How about:
Did you have fun today?
How did you play?
How did you feel about your playing today?
Did you achieve your goals today?
Any question oriented towards effort and enjoyment, rather than winning or losing, is desirable. Do you know of parents (you perhaps?) who take their children to McDonald's/Pizza Hut/Dairy Queen after a game? Many of us do, but does it matter whether your child won or lost? If it doesn't, great! If it does, then this is a behavior that should change. Going out to eat after a game should be contingent on having done one's best, not having won or lost.

Success

Chapter 7 provides some very poignant feedback from our children about what they like and don't like about sports, but also the good and bad things that parents sometimes do. Many of the children talk about pressure and criticism from parents, and an emphasis on winning. We must be careful about the verbal, and nonverbal, messages we send to our children about winning. That look after the game when your child or the team has lost can be worth a thousand words. We hope that you agree with our philosophical approach here, and that your words and actions will follow that attitude of emphasizing doing one's best.

Strategies for Constructive Communication

A key to success is constructive communication. For parents to become more encouraging with their children, they have to be able to talk with them, so the children know they are being listened to. Communication is a fundamental ingredient in enhancing relationships.

Communication represents the ability of a parent (or, for that matter, a coach) to pay attention, listen, perceive, and respond verbally or nonverbally to a child. As parents, some of us may be comfortable in quickly resolving challenges with our children. We do not see the need to allow our children to express themselves. Furthermore, some parents may not be comfortable with expressing feelings, especially when it may cause emotional discomfort with their children as well as within themselves. Some families may not recognize the benefit of open communication and how it enhances relationships.

The following information will be valuable as approaches which will help you problem solve with your children. These techniques will be more effective with children who are nine years old and older. The techniques should help parents recognize that responding to the emotional needs of their children may be more effective than reacting. In fact, many parents find that their children will more frequently seek them out as a consequence of feeling more comfortable. Clinical research points out that communication problems are a major deficit in interpersonal relationships. Most family problems stem from misunderstandings as well as ineffective communication. The outcome usually results in frustration and anger among all members involved.

Many adults recognize behaviors (verbal and nonverbal) they use or are aware of which promote conversation as opposed to less helpful strategies. For example, most children and adults respond more comfortably in communicating with another when the individual demonstrates that s/he is trying to listen more attentively, is not interrupting, and is sitting in an open and relaxed fashion. People also feel more comfortable when they perceive a genuine sense of concern, respect, encouragement, empathy, and acceptance.

On the other hand, communication is often suppressed when children are constantly given advice (rather than listened to), when the listener blames, becomes too demanding, and possibly strays too much from the topic or only gives examples of how s/he thinks the problem should be handled. Additionally, the relationship is also negatively impacted when the listener nonverbally demonstrates a lack of interest. Examples which illustrate nonverbal lack of interest or genuineness are when the listener's body position is rigid and tense, the individual avoids proper eye contact, or when the listener's body posture is either too rigid or slouching.

An excellent approach to enhancing the dialogue between parent and child is known as responsive listening. This strategy is defined as attending and responding accurately and sensitively to the verbal and nonverbal messages that are coming from the child. Parents need to learn to not only respond to the content of what a child is saying, but also respond to the child's feelings. We must take our time and respond correctly to the child's complete message. We need to integrate the content of the child's message with the underlying feelings.

In trying to respond to the child's feelings, we must not only be aware of what the child is saying verbally, but also pay attention to what the child is expressing nonverbally (postural and facial expressions). Sometimes there is a tremendous difference in what is being said and the nonverbal behaviors. This contradictory information may lead to selecting an inaccurate assumption. Clarification may be needed to really get to the root of the child's issues. These nonverbal expressions tell us a great deal about how the child is handling the experience. The child's tone of voice as well as facial expressions are also invaluable sources.

For example, a child may say to his/her parents after coming home from a game, "Things are not going so good for me. Not on the field, not with my teammates, and not with the coach. I don't feel I am holding up my part of the bargain and I feel like a failure. I want to quit." What is the child trying to tell us? The main theme of the conversation suggests that the child feels very down. She is feeling very discouraged because she thinks everything on the team is falling apart, especially as it relates to her. As a parent, if you were in her position, wouldn't you also feel very dejected?

To develop a responsive statement, a parent will have to integrate two components. In the first part of our response, we will formulate a statement that accurately integrates what we perceive the child feels. We must try and select a feeling word which is the most accurate both in intensity as well as actual feeling. We may do this by using a simple "You feel _____" formulation.

To assist in developing a more comprehensive "feeling" vocabulary, parents may want to practice formulating at least 5-10 feeling words for the feeling states of sadness, happiness, anxiety, shame, and anger. For example, other words for sadness could be demoralized, dejected, distressed, lousy, and lonely. On the other hand, the word angry could also be expressed as feeling annoyed, furious, mad, and enraged. To be effective, the feeling vocabulary needs to feel comfortable to the parent. That is why we suggest if you want to practice responsive listening, you should try to develop a vocabulary which best suits your personality.

The second part of the response, after identifying how the child feels, is putting the feeling together with the content of the child's statements. The content gives meaning to the child's expressions of the experiences. Remember the feelings that you just identified are about the content. The content provides the reason for the child feeling the way s/he does.

The formula one uses after formulating the feeling component of a sentence (e.g., You feel _____) is to immediately follow the statement "You feel......" by "because _____). Now you have been able to capture both the feeling and the content of what the child has said.

Using responsive listening allows a parent to attempt to read the mind of a child by first clarifying how the child feels as well as clarifying the content that was shared. Returning to our first example, the parent may respond that, "You feel demoralized because everything seems to be going wrong for you on the team."

What is exciting about this approach is that when you are correct, children feel understood and are encouraged to clarify and continue talking. When you are incorrect, children tend to notice your genuineness in communicating and are willing to modify your statement and continue opening up. We will now add a few more strategies which complement responsive listening and help parents encourage more optimal discussions with their children.

1. *Paraphrasing*—This approach is used when a parent attempts to rephrase what a child has said. Sometimes this is

very helpful, especially when the child may not be clear and a parent wants clarification.

2. *Probing*—Some people do not realize that it is helpful to ask children questions to get more information. Unfortunately, they ask closed-ended questions which only require a yes or no answer. It is helpful for parents to use open-ended probes such as "Tell me about your day," or "What do you think of...."

3. *Redirecting or Summarizing*—It is impossible to always be reflective when talking to our children. At times we may need to ask questions or redirect the discussion. That is entirely appropriate. Once that occurs, parents can return to applying the strategies we already have noted. Lastly, it is imperative for parents to realize that it is extremely helpful while communicating to summarize what has already been stated, and review the highlights. This lets the child know what has been previously discussed and ascertains if any clarification is needed.

Effective communication may be more natural for some parents than others. What is important is that parents respect and recognize the value of listening and responding to their child's emotions. In a child's quest to secure the most exciting, and successful sporting activity, children need to be heard and supported. Responsive listening is one avenue that will help parents reach their child.

A Developmental Perspective: What Should Parents Expect?

Throughout this chapter we have emphasized various definitions of *success*. We have also suggested how parents can view success. We also need to offer an understanding of how families can be helpful to their children in developing a "successful winning lifestyle." Parents will not be able to influence all dimensions. However, we should try and control what is in our power.

The home environment is crucial as a foundation. Children

who are more encouraged, and feel that their parents are supportive, will feel more at ease. Some children have parents who enjoy watching them play sports and do not put pressure on them to win all the time. These parents are encouraging and keep the game in perspective. They also do not focus on the outcome of games. The family discussions do not pertain to the child and his/her excellence (or lack of) on and off the field.

Younger Athletes

Parents of younger children need to set an example for their children. When parents demonstrate anxiety, and place a great deal of pressure on the outcome of a game, then their children may follow suit. Parents with children who are quite young, approximately four to eight years of age, should be very sensitive about how the children enjoy the game. If the child is ambivalent or fearful, parents must try and put these fears to rest. They should not always demand that the child continue participating just because s/he signed up.

We recall an incident when a seven-year-old boy was signed up by his parents to play soccer. After the parents purchased all the equipment and the child went to the first practice he was very unhappy. He went to the coach and told him that he did not want to play. The coach questioned his decision and asked the boy if his parents talked to him before they registered him for the sport. The little boy's response was simple. He said they told me, but they did not ask!

The first step, therefore, is to ask if the child is interested in playing the sport. It is essential that the child play because s/he wants to, not because it is the parents' favorite sport. Once the child makes a commitment, though, especially to a team, it is generally advisable to stick with it until the season is over. This is a good opportunity to learn about teamwork. The reasons offered by the child for not wanting to play may be things that can be corrected, such as fear of getting hit by the ball, not liking the coach's style, and so on.

Parents who are supportive would also try and help their children informally by practicing the skills at home (e.g., pitching and hitting, and trying to make it fun). They would also try to help the child feel comfortable as a member of a team and emphasize the group/social aspect of participation. At this age FUN is the key element, along with playing with and making new friends and learning skills.

Older Athletes

As the child ages (older than nine years of age), parents must continue to listen closely to their child. Parents should continue to be supportive, and should be ready to help if asked in dealing with issues such as peer pressure, competing interests, and so on. However, they should not push or discourage their child by placing unreasonable demands or pressure. They should be listeners rather than doers.

Responsive listening, as noted earlier, is a strategy that is a welcome asset to parents. Responsive listening enhances communication and encourages further discussion. Too often parents either solve their children's challenges or just give advice. Older children need parents who listen to them and who are also willing to allow them to own their problems.

As noted in Chapter 2, as children age the pressures can increase. Parents need to help their children put sports into perspective. If parents find their children becoming anxious, they need to solve this with their children by offering solutions. In Chapter 6, we will note some relaxation strategies which children can learn.

The ultimate value to the child is the way the parent views "success" and how the parent communicates that belief system to the child. If a parent develops a healthy outlook and actually lives it, the child will feel supported. William Allen Drumgoold highlights in his famous poem, "The Bridge Builder," that the greatest gift that we can be to our children is to become their bridge builder. As he elegantly states at the end of the poem, "A youth's feet must pass this way. He too must cross in the twilight dim, good friend I build the bridge for him."

Parents are bridge builders and can be very helpful to their children in accessing opportunities. This access does not guarantee success, but rather an opportunity. As parents, our role should be considered as sustaining our children in experiencing success and enjoyment in sport. Success is not reflected on the scoreboard. It is reflected in our hearts and minds.

Your Child's Bill of Rights

One thing we can do is ensure that we support a Bill of Rights for Young Athletes. The Bill of Rights (See Appendix 2) is one that will ensure success in youth sports for your children—and for you. We hope that you will read the Bill of Rights carefully and subscribe to the philosophy espoused in it.

Changing the Way We "Keep Score"

Are there ways we can de-emphasize the role that winning has in organized sports? Absolutely! Many leagues have had success doing things like eliminating standings (of teams), not keeping score during games, and not keeping batting averages and statistics for players (at least in terms of comparing them team/league wide). What does the league your child plays in do? Are standings and playoffs an important topic of conversation for parents? Does this matter to your children? We have been socialized to think in terms of winning and losing, and it is admittedly not easy to shift from that base. But we can make that shift by making changes such as those noted above—anything that de-emphasizes outcome and emphasizes performance— playing one's hardest, doing one's best, all in the spirit of good sportsmanship and having fun, is the real success story.

Achieving Your Goals

In Chapter 6 we address some areas within psychological skills training, including goal setting. Tied into doing your best and putting out 100% is the idea of achieving your goals. While this can be related to achieving one's potential, it is really more in line with having set challenging, but realistic goals (more on that in Chapter 6), and needing to work hard to achieve those. If the goals are set appropriately, then hard work will result in achieving them. We all set goals in many areas of our lives. Setting goals and working hard to achieve them in youth sports is an exceptionally rewarding experience and provides, in the end, for a very successful experience.

Being Successful

In the end, what does being successful mean? Being successful means supporting your child, making sure that your child knows that having fun and doing one's best are the primary elements that you want to focus upon in participating in sports. Learning skills, getting exercise, enjoying competition, and all the other factors are important and come with the "territory." However, the emphasis on FUN and doing one's best will take you and your children a long way towards a successful experience in sports!

Chapter 5

What to Look for in a Coach:
The Parent as Educated Consumer

When we shop for a car, most of us do a great deal of homework—we read consumer reviews, check with friends, test drive various models, etc. We want to be sure that we are purchasing the best car available. Similarly, when we make a decision to have our children participate in youth sports, we should be doing just as intensive and extensive a search.

A youth sports experience can have a significant effect on a child—usually positive but occasionally negative. To try and ensure that the scales are tilted towards the positive, checking out the various leagues in your area is an important first step. We reviewed the kinds of things one should look for in assessing a league in Chapter 2, the flavorful Baskin-Robbins chapter.

Let's assume that you've selected the league you want (or perhaps you don't have a choice if only one league is available in your area). The next critical question is: "Who will be my child's coach?" Hopefully you will have a choice in this matter. If yes, the following information will help in the selection process. If no, the following information will still be helpful, but only in terms of what positives/negatives to look for. Most coaches are well meaning, if not skilled at coaching, and one can generally find positives with most coaches.

Occasionally, however, for some coaches (a small minority, but still a number large enough to concern us!) the negatives are sufficiently great that we choose not to enroll our child in a program. Rather, it seems better to spend the time in informal play, or doing other things, than being subjected to the influence of a particularly negative coach. Coaches who yell and scream too much, who continually criticize their athletes (our children!), or engage in dangerous coaching practices are ones who fall to the bottom of the positivity chart (or come to the top of the negativity chart, if you prefer).

Coach John was an example of this. Coach John was a youth baseball coach, and thought that the way to motivate his players was to yell and scream at them, and continually criticize them for every little mistake made, with the idea of motivating them to do well. Curiously, though, he never seemed to praise them when they did well! Perhaps he thought the players would feel they were indeed doing well and rest on their laurels, not working hard enough. This professional model of coaching, or at least what Coach John thought he saw on television and at the ballpark, got results with a few players, but most of his players were unhappy and did not like being treated the way they were. The negative experience led many of them to give up baseball at the end of the season. The final section of this chapter, educating the coach, will be helpful in overcoming negatives, such as with Coach John.

It is important to remember that you are generally talking with volunteer coaches, who are giving their time and not expecting to get grilled with many questions. The questions at the end of this chapter are offered as suggestions—you should modify them and add or subtract questions to meet your needs. You may be a volunteer coach yourself, or have served as one in the past. Asking questions in a supportive, positive manner will come across much better than a grilling.

Choosing a Coach

The choice of a coach for your child is a critical one. You, as parents, are entrusting this coach with the physical, psychological, and skill development of your child in sports. In our society the coach has an exalted position, and children and adolescents often look up to the coach as an almost omniscient figure. Although this view of the coach is changing somewhat these days, it is still generally true. Accordingly, we must gather as much information as we can before choosing a coach to ensure that we make the right decision.

Unfortunately, the first difficulty we may encounter is the lack of a choice! In many situations, your child will be assigned to a team based on where you live, by luck of the draw, or by selection by a group of coaches. You may at least be able to choose the type of league in which your child plays (note our earlier discussion in Chapter 2), but you may have little choice beyond that aspect of participation.

If this is the case, you can then use the following guidelines to decide whether your child should play for this coach *at all*—it may be better to find other options than to play for a "bad" coach. You *do* have a choice in that case as well, even though, for your child, not playing may not seem like much of a choice at all.

You are the Consumer

Remember that *you are the consumer*—you do have a choice about the kind of league in which your child plays and the coach for whom your child plays. Your child *does not* have to play for someone who does not have the capabilities to meet your expectations and those of your child. There are, fortunately, many

What to Look for in a Coach

options available for participation at different levels, in many different sports, and you and your child want the best experience possible. Shop around for a league/coach with the characteristics you want. You are entrusting the care of your child to this coach—be certain that you know what you are getting!

Coaching Background

The two areas of greatest importance in choosing a coach are background (academic preparation, coaching experience, playing experience) and philosophy. Let's explore each area in detail.

Background: Academic Preparation

Ideally, a coach will have some academic preparation for the position of coach. This may include college degree(s) in fields such as physical education/kinesiology/exercise and sport sciences with major or minor emphases in coaching. Coursework in coaching, teaching/pedagogy, first aid, and the sport sciences (sport psychology, motor learning, exercise physiology, biomechanics, etc.) are highly desirable.

Unfortunately, many coaches do not have this depth of training. Many have, however, taken workshops or had other educational experiences such as those offered by ASEP (the American Sport Education Program) or PACE (Program And Coaching Effectiveness). These programs offer training in selected areas such as sport psychology, exercise physiology, and motor skill development for a modest number of hours, but at least provide a basic background in these areas. Please check the list of resources in the back of this book for more information on these programs.

This academic preparation provides a knowledge base that makes for a more effective coach. Each of the academic areas offers knowledge that is critical for an effective coach—the psychological aspects of participation (sport psychology, motor learning, motor skill development, coaching skills) as well as the physical aspects of participation (exercise physiology, biomechanics, first aid). Coaches with this academic background generally also get some "continuing education," just as many of us have to do for our professions to keep current in our field. Taking additional and/or advanced courses, attending workshops, belonging to coaching associations, and reading coaching journals are all excellent ways of keeping up with advancements and knowledge in the field. Is the coach doing any or all of these?

All things being equal, a coach with this knowledge base would be preferred over one who does not have this background. Having this knowledge base, of course, doesn't always mean the coach uses this knowledge effectively. Get information about the coach's academic background and how the coach uses this background to make him/herself a more effective coach.

Background: Coaching Experience

What sort of coaching experience does the coach have? Is this the seventh season in this league for this coach or is the coach a first-timer at this or any other level? A new coach may have worked in fewer (perhaps no) situations and have less of a grasp of what being a coach really means than an experienced coach with many years in the sport.

Experience at other levels (such as high school or college) is helpful, as long as the philosophy that comes with the coach is appropriate to the level in which your child is playing. A youth league is no place for a coach who still carries a "professional," "win at all costs" philosophy. Additionally, there are differences in ability between those who play in a youth league, high school, or college players. The coach must have the patience and the skills to work with and teach youth league players after experience at higher skill levels. This patience and the skills needed are not always present. In major league baseball, for example, it is rare to see ex-star players be successful as managers. These star players often have difficulty working with players with lesser skill levels, and can't make the adjustment to this lower ability level. Make sure that your child's coach doesn't fall into this category.

The experience at different levels ties into the competitive/cooperative element we discussed earlier. Experience in only a competitive environment may make it hard for a coach to make the transition to a cooperatively oriented league. Similarly, a coach oriented towards a cooperative framework may find it difficult to be successful in a competitively oriented league. Even experience at a competitive level does not mean that a "professional," "win at all costs" philosophy is necessary. The word *success* can mean many different things. Chapter 4 was devoted to a definition of success and what this term really means. For the moment, find out what levels the coach has worked at as well as with what degree of success at these levels.

How do you measure coaching success? In competitive leagues, win/loss record is one measure, but it really is a minor one at younger age levels. More importantly, are there any measures of how many players went on to play in future years? How many players played for high school/college teams? One of the most important questions one can ask is how the players improved in performance over the season, although this information is not always available. However, this information is important enough to ask parents of players from previous years how the coach is at getting the best out of the players and how much improvement the players made during the season. The most important question one can ask, in line with our philosophy and appropriate for both competitive and cooperative leagues, is whether the players had *fun*—did they enjoy their experience? This information can also be asked of parents of players from previous years.

How do we measure improvement in a cooperatively oriented league? A key question is, just as in the competitive league, how the players improved in performance over the season. Given that this information is not always available (you could, as suggested, ask parents of players from previous years), other key questions can be asked:

How much fun did the players have?

Did the players' social skills improve?

Did the players' self-esteem increase during the season?

Did the players return the following season?

Research shows that coaches who behave more positively towards their players tend to have players who come back the next season than coaches who behave more negatively. The players of the negative coaches tend to drop out and either seek other sport opportunities or no sport at all!

This experience at different levels ties in with experience with athletes of different ages. There is a world of difference between seven-year-olds and 15-year-olds. Developmental issues with respect to physical, psychological, and skill areas are different at different ages. Coaches who have experience and understand the appropriate developmental level for the age they will be working with are vastly preferable to coaches with no experience at this age. One can ask the coach about experience with children the same age as your child, but the under-

What to Look for in a Coach

standing component may need to be discovered by asking parents of children who have had the coach in previous years.

Experience in the sport is also important. Although any experience may be better than no experience, a coach with experience in football trying to serve as a Little League baseball coach may have a tough time, especially initially. Similarly, a swim coach may have trouble adjusting to coaching a hockey team. Ideally, the coach will have experience in the sport, particularly at the level in which your child is playing. One way experience can be gotten is by working as an assistant coach for a while before becoming the head coach.

Experience across a multicultural spectrum can also be important—does the coach have experience with both boys and girls, and with children of different racial and ethnic backgrounds? This experience may be helpful in working with children with varied backgrounds as well as interacting with you, the parents. The coach who is knowledgeable about and sensitive towards these issues associated with a diverse group of players (and parents) will be that much more successful. Get information about the coach's coaching background and how the coach uses this background to make him/herself a more effective coach.

Background: Playing Experience

Given that coaches usually have experience playing the sport being coached, what kind of experience does the coach have? Playing recreationally on the playgrounds or baseball fields with one's friends is not the same as playing organized sports at the high school or collegiate levels, or even the professional ranks. The coach with more experience will have been in many more game situations, different circumstances, worked/played with different coaches and players, and potentially will be better able to be an effective coach than someone who has not had these kinds of experiences.

A factor related to playing experience is talent or skill level. Just as with the baseball manager example earlier, we often hear about successful managers or coaches not being the superstars but being the bench or role players. Think about it—how many professional (or even college/university) coaches were superstar athletes? How many superstar athletes have tried their hands at coaching and failed? The non-superstar may have had to work harder, spent more time studying the nuances of the game, had to "really" learn the game in order to be successful. This wealth of experience is invaluable when a coaching role is assumed years later. The glamour associated with a "superstar" coach may not always be reflected in how the coach works with children.

Finding out what levels of experience your potential coach has had and the role the coach played at that level is important. The coach may enjoy talking about past playing experiences. If you listen carefully, you may gain insights as to the kind of experiences the coach had and the kind of player the coach was. You might find out what type of coach the current (potential) coach had when s/he was playing and how the current coach views this person now. These stories will tell you a lot about the kind of coach this person will be and the kinds of experiences the coach will provide for your child. Get information about the coach's playing experience and how the coach uses this background to make him/herself a more effective coach.

Philosophy

"Winning isn't everything, it's the only thing."

"Show me a good loser and I'll show you a loser."

You've all heard quotes like these. Some of you may even believe these sentiments. If so, you're probably not going to like the next few paragraphs. As you saw in Chapter 4, we don't believe that winning is "the only thing," but we would agree that "trying to win is," as the famous sport psychologist Rainer Martens once said. We define *success* as trying your best, putting forth 100% effort, doing the best that you can. Success does *not* equal winning in our playbook. The key question is how the coach views success—what is his/her philosophy about working with your children to facilitate their success?

Select a coach who believes in the definition of success that we've tried to encourage you to adopt—putting forth your best every time you play. Doing our best, giving 100%, is all we, and our coaches, can realistically ask for. A coach with a similar definition of success is one whom we would support.

Watching the coach in action can often be very helpful—we've all seen people who say one thing and act differently. While the coach may have the best of intentions, and offer a philosophical approach to coaching with which you agree whole-heartedly, perhaps the coach acts differently once the game starts and the coach gets caught up in the spirit and the action of the game or when adults are not around.

This makes planning ahead, if possible, highly desirable. See the coaches in action in the league in which you're interested. Just as coaches sometimes scout future players, you can scout future coaches. You may see some in action whom you can rule out even before talking with them. Others may appear to be just what you're looking for, and meeting with them would be desirable. This is a helpful step for you and your child in deciding where to play and for whom in the coming season. Get information about the coach's coaching philosophy and how the coach uses this background to make him/herself a more effective coach. The next section on philosophy and behavior provides some examples of behaviors we look for in coaches for our children.

Philosophy and Behavior

While a coach's philosophy is important, the critical factor is, of course, behavior. Does the coach practice what s/he preaches?

Does the coach walk the talk, as some would say? A coach who professes belief in doing one's best and giving 100% as being the keys to success, and then *behaves* as if winning and losing are what's important, is not making the link between philosophy  (attitude) and behavior. This attitude/behavior link has been explored extensively in psychology. People don't always do (behave) what they say/believe/think. Research suggests that the link between attitude and behavior is generally relatively weak, although the strength of the link is greater depending on various factors which are beyond the scope of this book. The critical factor is the coach's behavior—does the coach practice what s/he preaches?

What kinds of things should the coach be doing (and what should the coach not be doing)? Behaviors the coach should be engaging in are positive in orientation:

1. Providing praise frequently for positive actions. These actions can be performance (a good play) or effort (good hustle, even if the outcome wasn't successful). The praise doesn't have to be continual (a steady stream of positive statements may actually become too much after a while and lose their meaning), but should be relatively frequent *and* contingent on performance/effort. Examples would be:

    a) Great play!

    b) Good hustle! Way to go after that ball!

    c) Nice try! You'll get it next time!

2. Providing technical instruction—teaching your children how to play the game is important. We often recommend what's called a sandwich—a positive comment about effort, followed by a technical instructional comment, followed by another positive comment. An example would be:

What to Look for in a Coach

> *a) Nice try on that grounder.*
>
> *b) Next time make sure your glove is positioned in front of you and you're blocking the ball's path with your body.*
>
> *c) You'll get the next one. Keep up the good effort!*

The "nice try" acknowledges an unsuccessful effort (the child knows s/he didn't make the play), but focuses on a positive aspect of performance (effort). The technical instruction suggests the way to do better next time. The closing positive comment reinforces the importance of doing one's best and, hopefully, being successful next time.

3. Focusing on FUN—the coach should be reinforcing enjoyment of the game. This could be mentioning things like what a great day it is to play, the fun of running around, the camaraderie of being with teammates, etc. This doesn't mean goofing around. But it does mean enjoying what you're doing—isn't that the reason for PLAYing a sport?!

4. Playing everyone! Did your child sign up to sit on the bench? We doubt it! Everyone should have, ideally, an equal opportunity to play. At the very least, everyone should play a substantial amount of time to make all the practice and travel time worthwhile. Children play sports to PLAY, not to sit. Children have said that they would rather play for a losing team than sit on the bench for a winning team. They want to play!

5. Giving players opportunities at different positions. Especially for younger players, providing opportunities to play different positions provides chances for action and experiences in discovering what they like best. Being designated right fielder for life is no fun! Rotating players during the season (or even during a game) can give multiple opportunities for action and learning experiences.

Behaviors the coach should *not* be engaging in are negative ones. The primary one we see is criticism. Many coaches feel that continually criticizing players: "That was terrible!" "Can't anyone here play this game?" "Where'd you learn to play like that?" (from you, coach?) and other such comments are the way to motivate players. They will serve to motivate players—right out the door, away from the sport.

This kind of coach never has anything good to say. This coach may think that praise will result in the players slacking off, but nothing could be further from the truth. None of us likes to continually hear, "No, no, no, you're not good enough," and on and on. Use the sandwich approach! Be positive! Praise your children whenever possible! Give us some positive feedback, coach, and we'll do anything for you!

Background Checks

We have talked extensively about coaching background. In today's society, unfortunately, there are individuals who violate the trust that parents and children place in them as coaches. We occasionally read in our newspapers about coaches who are arrested for sexual abuse of children. Issues of voyeurism are occasionally present in coaches as well. Some leagues require background checks of coaches to ensure that they do not have a history, at least a legally established one, of child sexual abuse. You may wish to check if your youth sports league has such a system of checks in place. Hopefully this is a situation your league will never encounter, but it does happen often enough to warrant caution.

Educating the Coach

What can you do to educate the coach, if you have someone who will be working with your children and you think the coach will be receptive to information that will help in being more effective? Some of the change can come from an increase in knowledge. Some of the programs in the resource list at the back (remember the ASEP and PACE programs) can be helpful for the coach who is positive but just needs more education.

What to Look for in a Coach

Don't forget resources in your area—there may be a sport psychologist who would be willing to talk with your youth sport league in general, or coach(es) in particular. Check your local college/university, sports medicine center, state psychology association referral network, or call/write/e-mail Michael Sachs at his number/address [noted at the end of the book] for a referral.

The coach who knows his/her stuff, but needs an attitude adjustment (!), may benefit from a frank discussion of philosophy, especially if there are league policies which address these issues. These policies may emphasize a participation focus rather than a win/loss focus. The coach may not be aware of these policies, or simply have forgotten these policies in falling back on past socialization experiences that emphasized a competitive orientation to sport. Some parents have videotaped practices and games and showed coaches what their behavior is really like. Coaches are sometimes surprised at this lack of correspondence between philosophy and behavior (note our comments earlier about the attitude/behavior link), and this may be enough to put them on notice to be more careful about what they say and do.

A frank discussion of expectations may be enough to reorient the coach. If not, adding assistant coaches (if some are available and/or allowed) may offset the more competitive/negative coach. There may be opportunities for you to assist as an assistant coach and help the coach be more effective.

Many leagues have grievance procedures that are effective. Working together with other parents as a group is also often more effective than parents working individually. A final, more drastic step may be to find a new coach!

Questions for the prospective coach:
1. What is your coaching background with respect to academic preparation, such as college/university coursework or workshops or other educational experiences?

2. What is your coaching background with respect to coaching experience, such as different age groups, different sports, and different types of leagues?
3. What is your playing experience in the sport you are coaching and other sports in which you have participated?
4. What is your coaching philosophy? What are some behaviors that you (the coach) engage in that are consistent with this philosophy?
5. How do you go about getting the best out of your athletes?
6. How do you define success?

Chapter 6

Psychological Skills Training

Sport psychology is best known for an emphasis on enhancing performance through Psychological Skills Training (PST), sometimes called Mental Training or Mental Toughness Training. In this chapter our interest is on five areas most often included within PST:

1) Goal Setting
2) Arousal Control (stress management/relaxation)
3) Imagery
4) Attention/Concentration
5) Positive Self-Talk

We have chosen to include some introductory information about this area to whet your appetite about sport psychology, and encourage you to pursue this area further through books (see bibliography for some suggestions) and contact with sport psychologists in your area. Some of the material will be presented from your perspective, rather than your child's per se.

The information can be applied fairly readily to your children, but will be particularly meaningful in relating to your own experiences.

There are some special considerations, however, in applying these skills with children. Although examining these considerations in depth is beyond the scope of this book, some of the books listed in the bibliography, particularly by Terry Orlick, will be very helpful. It is important to note that PST can be used not only to enhance athletic performance, but also performance in other settings such as school and work.

Goal Setting

An old Chinese saying notes that: "A journey of a thousand miles begins with a single step." This saying highlights the long journey that our children take between their current place in life and where they would like to be in sports (as well as school, work, social/family relationships, etc.) tomorrow, next week, next year, and further down the road. Pursuit of our goals encompasses two important aspects: the strength/intensity with which we pursue these goals, and the direction these steps/this journey takes us.

It may help to illustrate the application of goal setting by identifying 13 principles of goal setting and providing an example of how each can be applied to sports participation. We'll use a girl named Rachel, 10 years old, who participates on a youth league baseball team.

1. Involve the child in the goal setting process. This is particularly important because it provides children with a sense of ownership. This sense of ownership comes from being involved in discussing and making decisions about the goals they will try to reach.

Example: Rachel discussed with the sport psychologist her goals of improving her fielding ability, hitting for a higher average this year than last season, and improving her strength. These were things that she wanted to improve upon.

2. Establish realistic but challenging goals. It is important to consider what your child can achieve in a given period of time. An experienced sport participant may only "realistically" be able to improve a small amount within a few weeks or months. While one can never be certain what is truly realistic (perhaps an improvement of five seconds in the pool could have been six seconds?), the coach and athlete can determine together what seems reasonable, yet is challenging (i.e., one second may be too easy, while 10 seconds may be too much).

Consideration of the child's "potential" is helpful in establishing goals. Potential encompasses a multitude of factors, from genetic make-up, to sport specific skills, to physical capabilities, to psychological skills and dimensions such as motivation. As mentioned earlier, we sometimes joke that to become an Olympic champion one must choose one's parents carefully! Although one's genes do play an important role in what one is capable of achieving, the other factors play a much more significant role in what level of performance one is capable of eventually reaching.

Establishing a hierarchy of goals is recommended. One approach is to have three goals: an acceptable goal, a challenging goal, and a dream goal. An acceptable goal is one that is possible to achieve because you have either already done it or come very close to it. A challenging goal is one that you can reach with much work. A dream goal may be "only a dream," but our dreams do sometimes come true and having them is a good idea.

Example: Rachel and her coach decided that hitting .350 this season was realistic, yet challenging. Rachel had hit .310 last season, and felt .325 was acceptable, .350 was challenging, and .400 was her dream goal.

3. Establish short, intermediate, and long-term goals. Successful goal setting assumes that being reinforced by achieving small steps along the long journey towards that long-term goal is extremely important. The 40 point (.310 to .350) improvement from last season will take a great deal of work, and may not be achievable until the end of the season. However, each workout, each week, each month, can provide small successes and indications that one is progressing towards one's long-term goal. It is critical, therefore, to have short-term and intermediate goals along the way that signal success, that one is progressing according to plan.

Example: The long-term goal of hitting .350 for the season would be met with short-term goals (within a few days), intermediate-term goals (within a few months), and long-term (the entire season) goals. Each of the goals had specific targets for increasing from the previous season's .310 to work towards the goal of .350.

4. Establish performance, not outcome goals. We have control over our own performance, but not over the outcome of competition with other individuals or teams. A runner, for example, may run the "race of her life," yet be beaten by someone who is faster than she is, or simply has an even better day. By focusing upon our performance, we define success by how *we* perform, which is under our control, rather than how someone else performs, which is not under our control.

Example: Rachel felt that she could improve her hitting to a .350 average. She felt that this might be good enough to help her team win more games and help her move to the next competitive level. Although the outcome (winning games) was important, the emphasis was on performance, which was all Rachel could control. Rachel's focus was still hitting as well as she could.

5. Establish positive goals. It is more productive to work towards something positive (i.e., keep glove on the ground to catch grounders, throw correctly, etc.) than away from something negative (i.e., don't be out of position, don't use incorrect form for throwing, etc.). The positive goal has a clear objective.

The negative one indicates what not to do, but not what should be done. Setting positive goals is much more successful.

Example: Rachel established several positive goals for today's workout, including getting in position and using correct form to field grounders at second base, as well as using proper form (i.e., stance, holding the bat) for hitting practice.

6. Establish specific and measurable goals. In order to determine whether you have achieved a goal, the goal must be specific and measurable. Noting that you will hit better is not specific enough. Saying you will be more motivated to play is hard to measure. It is best to stick with goals that you can evaluate—hit a home run, field all balls cleanly, and so on. Establishing specific and measurable goals allows you to say clearly whether these goals have been achieved.

Example: Rachel decided to field 25 grounders today using correct form. She also decided to take 25 swings at the plate to work on her hitting and hit the ball cleanly 90% of the time.

7. Write the goals down. Writing down the goals provides a concrete record of what you hope to accomplish. This serves as a motivating force for working towards one's goal, and also provides reinforcement when a goal has been achieved. This achievement can be duly noted in the written record.

Example: Rachel had written that she expected to hit .350 by the end of the season. Noting this in her written log made her feel good about accomplishing her hitting goals every week (which she wrote down and kept track of after each hitting session).

8. Identify target dates. Part of establishing specific goals is specifying when you expect to complete these goals. It is important to specify target dates for each of the goals you are striving to accomplish.

Example: Rachel will work on her hitting for two hours per week—one half hour on Monday, Tuesday, Thursday, and Friday. Rachel will begin the season where she left off the previous season, at .310, then increase 10 points each month thereafter for the four months of the season.

9. *Establish individual and team goals.* Individual goals are important for determining whether your children are achieving levels of performance of which they are capable. If your child is participating on a team, then team goals are also important to provide a measure of how well the team is doing in progressing towards meeting its potential.

Example: Rachel had established individual performance goals for hitting and fielding. In baseball a team can establish goals for batting average, scoring runs, fielding percentage, earned run average, and so on.

10. *Establish practice and competition goals.* Goals are important both for practice situations, which occur frequently, and competition, which occurs less frequently. Each practice should have clearly defined goals as to what you expect to accomplish in the time available. These practice sessions then bear fruit at competition, when goals for performance are also important to assess one's level of achievement.

Example: Goals for practice included fielding drills (i.e., number of grounders/repetitions, turning the double play, etc.) and hitting (i.e., taking batting practice—25 swings per player, hitting behind the runner). Goals for games included batting average, fielding the ball cleaning, making accurate throws, holding the opponents to two runs in the game, and so on.

11. *Reevaluate the goals periodically.* On a regular basis your goals should be reviewed to be certain that they are still realistic, yet challenging. Sometimes you progress more quickly then expected, other times more slowly. Reevaluating your goals on a regular basis allows you to keep them realistic, yet challenging.

Example: Rachel evaluated her goals every few weeks to make sure that she wasn't overtraining in an attempt to keep up with an unrealistic set of expectations, nor undertraining because the goals she had set were too "easy." She decided that the ones she had set were on target and she maintained them.

12. *Support the goals.* It is important for others, especially you, the parents, to support the goals that have been developed by your child, usually in conjunction with the coach. This form of social support helps the athlete maintain focus on the goals, secure in the knowledge that this is the right direction to take.

Example: Rachel regularly reviewed her goals with her coach, and continually received encouragement that she was progressing well and was achieving realistic, yet challenging levels of performance for her.

13. *Establish SMART goals:*

        Specific

        Measurable

        Appropriate

        Realistic

        Time Bound

This acronym is an easy one for many athletes to remember, including many of the key elements of goal setting and reinforcing the desire that most of us have, to be SMART—smart people have smart goals.

In summary, goal setting is a critical element in athletic performance, providing a motivational framework within which the athlete plots a direction and a level of intensity for progressing towards improving performance.

Arousal Control

Arousal control is a general term that covers what we might call "stress management" or "relaxation." Arousal is, for our purposes, a continuum of physical and psychological activation. Our level of arousal, or activation, can range from sleep to a manic state ("bouncing off the walls"). More practically, it can range from boredom or disinterest (i.e., a boring lecture, a television show in which we have no interest, an opponent whom we "know" we can beat easily) to high levels of activity and intense focus on an upcoming opponent, event, or activity.

The most popular view of the arousal continuum is the inverted-U model (Figure 1)—which suggests that when arousal is too low (the person is underaroused) or too high (the person is overaroused), performance suffers (i.e., is low). When arousal is at some middle point, performance is at its maximum. This is often called "optimal arousal" or the optimal zone of functioning. The concept is that optimal performance occurs at this optimal state/level of arousal. Although there are other theoretical approaches to this area, the inverted-U model is the most useful for our discussion here.

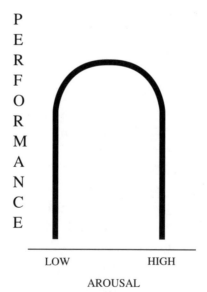

Figure 1
Inverted-U Model of Arousal

Psychological Skills Training

The inverted-U model is both person- and sport-specific. Each individual is different and, therefore, the point at which optimal arousal translates into optimal performance depends on the person and his/her skill level, experience, and so on. You know that you and your children are different from other parents and other children in different activities and different settings.

Each sport has its own arousal demands—for example, a much lower level of arousal is required of a golfer or archer than a defensive lineman in football or a runner. Within sports, different positions may require differing levels of arousal (in football, for example, different levels between a quarterback, a defensive lineman, and a kicker). Underarousal may lead to impaired concentration and an inability to call upon physical and psychological resources when needed during competition. Overarousal may result in similar effects, but additionally may prove debilitating in draining the person with a continuing state of tension and distractibility.

It requires a high degree of self-awareness to understand one's level of arousal and then also to remember those times when one performed best and what one's level of arousal was. It helps to remember, as well, the environmental conditions, the level/type of training, one's personal/work existence, etc.—all the factors that could contribute to improved (or decreased) performance.

Rachel had learned a number of strategies to regulate her arousal. When she was underaroused, she would warm up a bit more vigorously, to get her body moving more strongly, to make her more intense. Sometimes she would listen to hard rock music to get her aroused as well. Other players used cue words/phrases such as "Get Psyched" or "Up."

Overarousal (too highly aroused or too "psyched up") is more common. Children sometimes get very anxious/nervous (overaroused!) before a game. There are effective strategies for dealing with overarousal—Rachel, for example, used relaxation strategies. The most effective were simple deep breathing exercises. These "calming down" exercises consisted of deep, diaphragmatic breathing, two-three times, and produced immediate effects. She found that these were useful in school as well (before giving a book report in front of the class). However, these had been learned and practiced over a long period of time. Others who didn't practice and just tried to breathe deeply when they were overly aroused didn't obtain the same effects. Other approaches available include neuromuscular relaxation and meditation. Some of the books in the bibliography (especially Terry Orlick's books) will help you follow up on this area if you are interested.

Imagery

Imagery is often thought of as "seeing in the mind's eye." It is the process of creating, or recreating, an experience in one's mind. The term *visualization* is often used instead of imagery, because most people focus primarily, or even only, upon the visual component of imagery. Ideally, imagery encompasses all the senses—visual, auditory (what you hear), smell, touch, gustatory (what you taste), as well as kinesthetic (how your body moves).

How does this work for Rachel as she images her upcoming baseball game? Rachel sees the field across town, including the dugout, the neighborhood, the nearby playground. She hears the sounds of other players, and spectators in the stands, coaches and umpires chatting on the side. She smells the scents of suburban Philadelphia, the trees and plants. She touches the grass next to her as she stretches before going for a warm-up jog in the outfield. She tastes the sweat on her upper lip. She feels the sensation of moving to field grounders cleanly during the game, and throwing the runners out easily.

You can imagine a similar image for yourself as you think of a past event (recreating an experience) or an upcoming event (creating an experience). Imaging in all the senses helps make images more *vivid*. Along with *controllability*, *vividness* is a key element in imagery training. You want to make your images as vivid, as realistic as possible. The image should be as close as possible to the actual experience—and, ideally, all the senses would be involved. Of course, part of the role of imagery is to transfer these images from one's mind to actual performance—the closer the images are to the real thing, the better the transfer.

Controllability encompasses controlling images so that the images do what you want the images to do. You can increase the heat and humidity of the scene (in preparation for summer in Philadelphia) or decrease it (playing in September, as the weather starts to cool off), change the scenery for different locations, the smells, the sounds for the different sites, change pitchers and pitching styles (more fastballs, sliders, etc.). To the degree that you can control the image you have created/recreated, the image becomes that much more realistic, and can transfer more effectively to actual performance. These two elements, vividness and controllability, are critical in effective imagery.

A final note—some people are great imagers, while others have great difficulty creating an image at all. Many children, although not all, are great at imaging, at using their imagination! Just as some of us are more skilled at hitting a backhand in tennis, others can't play well at all. We all have differing skill levels, and it just takes some knowledge and practice to get to the point where this area (and the other PST areas) will be helpful. Imagery, as all the other psychological skills, can be learned.

Attention/Concentration

"Concentrate." "Focus." Rachel would often hear teammates and coaches yell this to her and other players. Focus is a common term for concentration, which derives from attention.

Attention is a process that directs our awareness as information becomes available to the senses. We start by being alert, by being aware of stimuli in the environment. Once we begin to attend to these stimuli, concentration enters as our ability to sustain attention on selected stimuli for a period of time. We sometimes call this "attention span." How long can you concentrate, or focus, on a particular stimulus (i.e., a television show, a book, an opposing player or fellow competitors) before your mind "wanders," before you have distracting thoughts, before you start thinking about other things?

How can we enhance our ability to concentrate? First, establish standard cues and mind sets to assist in attending to task relevant cues. On the rare occasions when Rachel found her mind wandering, she could refocus on the game with one word or cue—PLAY.

Second, practice—provide opportunities to develop the ability to sustain concentration. Rachel used exercises during practice to build her attentional skills, focusing on the batter and the ball at all times when she was in the field, not attending to distracting sounds and other environmental input, but focusing on the game. Playing attentional games, such as trying to focus while others might try to distract you, can be an enjoyable way to practice this skill.

Third, practice attention shifting exercises. Rachel's practice sessions also involved shifting between focusing on a range of stimuli from broad to narrow, which we categorize as width, to a range from internal to external, which we call direction. Width ranges from broad (a great deal of stimuli, such as a quarterback might have to deal with on the field or a coach considers when preparing a game plan) to narrow (a limited amount of stimuli, from rehearsing one's tennis backhand to concentrating on making that 10-foot putt). Direction ranges from internal (using imagery to mentally rehearse your positioning in the batter's box) to external (focusing "only" on the pitcher and the ball that will be coming to the plate to be hit). These can be combined to form four general attentional styles: broad-internal (analyzing—as in the coach preparing a game plan with a lot of options), broad-external (assessing—as in a quarterback assessing the field in front of him/her), narrow-external (performance—as in the batter getting ready to hit), and narrow-internal (rehearsal—as in the shortstop mentally rehearsing fielding the ball cleanly and throwing the runner out at first base). Many sports, such as football, hockey, soccer, and baseball, involve switching among these styles quickly, and practicing this switching ability can be extremely helpful in enhancing performance. This concept of attentional styles was developed by noted sport psychologist Robert Nideffer—more about this area and other PST skills can be found in the references in the bibliography.

Fourth, Rachel developed a pre-event (pre-performance) routine that worked for her. She would use some quiet time to listen to a calming tape (with sounds of the sea shore) and image playing her best. She would then go through her stretching and warm-up routine to be ready to play. This pre-event routine provided a comfortable routine that got her physically and psychologically primed, yet didn't require any decision making or focusing upon distracting elements within the environment. Her teammates had their own routines, but each one was different—the routine needs to be personalized (i.e., different strokes for different folks).

Finally, as will be seen in more detail in the next section on self-talk, Rachel had a specific cue to stop any negative thoughts that might enter her mind during the game or stop her mind from wandering if she found herself drifting off (baseball games sometimes can be "slow"). As soon as she attended to these thoughts, as noted above, she would say the word PLAY to herself. This served, after much practice, to immediately direct her attention away from these other thoughts and onto the game at hand.

Rachel found that there were always distractions before and during games, and that it was sometimes easy to lose her concentration. Practicing this psychological skill allowed her to develop it into a strength and she was known in baseball circles as a very focused person on the diamond.

Self-Talk

"We are not disturbed by things, but rather the view we take of them." (Epictetus)

"There is nothing either good or bad, but thinking makes it so." (Shakespeare)

The perception we have of things that occur in the world leads to our thoughts and feelings, and what we say to ourselves and others. This perception, or evaluation, of some real or imagined environmental stimulus (stimuli) leads to our interpretation of these events. This interpretation is accompanied or followed by some response—emotional, physiological, and perhaps behavioral. These feelings and reactions may be presented in the form of self-talk, actual verbal statements that others can hear, or words we say to ourselves that we can "hear" very clearly.

The question, of course, is what "direction"—positive or negative—this self-talk takes. Positive self-talk—"I feel strong today." "I have prepared well for this game." "I've worked hard in training." "I'm going to put out 100% effort today and do the best I can."—is desirable. It puts us in a positive frame of mind and has the potential to direct the body towards maximum performance.

Negative self-talk—"It's cold today. I'm not sure I can play well." "I'm feeling a bit tired today." "Oh no! There's Jim—I can't seem to get a hit off of him." "My legs are a bit sore today. Perhaps I won't be able to play well."—is undesirable. The old saying of "If you think you can't, you won't" applies here. Negative thinking leads to less than maximal performance—reduced effort, hesitancy in making key moves (taking the extra base), distraction, and so on. This lack of confidence, and lowered self-esteem, often leads to a self-fulfilling prophecy. One has doubts that one will do well, effort is affected, as is performance, all combining to confirm the original doubts about ability.

This vicious cycle must be attacked early and vigorously. Unfortunately, we often have long histories of negative self-talk, self-doubt that has developed over the years. Children have this less often, but it is still present in many of our children. Fortunately, there are ways of combating this negative self-talk. If you're one of the very few who never engage in negative self-talk (and your child doesn't either!), then congratulations—feel free to move on to the next section. However, if you're like the vast majority of us and at least occasionally engage in negative self-talk, please read on.

The first step is retrospection. You need to notice yourself engaging in negative self-talk. When do you do this? What do you say to yourself? Perhaps you find that before games you question your abilities—"I'm not sure I've trained enough." Or "I don't think I'm as good as the other players here (when actually you are)."—Or worry about the conditions—"Wow, it's sure cold today. I know I won't play well." Or "Lots of stones on the field—I don't like those. I'm sure I will field poorly."

Once you've answered these questions, self-monitoring is the next step. You need to be able to catch yourself engaging in negative self-talk so that you can then stop this process.

The third step is thought-stopping. The idea is to stop the negative thoughts by concentrating briefly on the undesired thought and then use a cue word or trigger to stop the thought and clear the mind. The cue word might be "Stop," or you might use a trigger such as snapping your finger. At this point, take a deep breath (remember the deep breathing discussed in the arousal control section), and then engage in positive self-talk. Use a positive, supportive statement, such as "I'm feeling strong today and will play well" or "I know the other pitcher and will hit well today." You are changing your thoughts from a negative mode of self-talk to a positive one!

Now that you will be using these positive statements, there are a few "rules" to remember in writing these:

1. Avoid negatives: don't say "I won't play poorly today," but say "I will play well today."
2. Keep the statement in the present tense, in the here-and-now: say "I feel strong."
3. Keep the statement in the first person (begin or refer to "I"): say "I will play well today."
4. Believe in the positive self-talk: don't say positive words just for the sake of saying these positive statements. If you don't believe you will do well, don't try to delude yourself. Above all you must be honest with yourself, but you can still be positive in evaluating your ability to perform and meet the goals you established earlier.

Quality, not Quantity

A final word about quality and quantity is important. The above material has focused upon the use of PST to enhance the *quantity* of participation in youth sports—performing better. PST can also be used to enhance the *quality* of sports participation. One can feel better about participating, and facilitate the feeling of fun and enjoyment that comes with doing something we/your children love and doing it well. There are many aspects to quality—restructuring goals for today to take a few moments to smell the flowers along the way, or using imagery to capture the smooth, flowing feeling of participation, or controlling arousal to enjoy the heightened sensation of the thrill of competition and testing yourself.

PST can be used to focus upon the enjoyment of participation as a means to an end—a healthy body and a healthy mind. Even if your children are elite athletes, they are hopefully participating for these reasons as well. Few of us participate in sport as a job (and even professional athletes hopefully enjoy it). Almost all of us participate because we love the sensation of playing hard and experiencing the joys of movement, of competing against ourselves and others, and the social camaraderie. In the end, we can say that we feel better physically and psychologically and we had fun.

Chapter 7

Children Speak Out

Many years ago there was a television show called "Kids Say the Darndest Things." The idea was that one would find words of wisdom in what children say that would make us laugh. Rather than laugh, or cry in some cases, we have found that our children do indeed tell us important things about what is good and bad about youth sports, and what we should be doing for them and with them. Accordingly, we decided to ask children in our neighborhoods, in California and in New Jersey/Pennsylvania, a few questions. We used a questionnaire for these youngsters, ages 6-14, who participate in organized youth sports (organized leagues in any sport, such as baseball, soccer, football, and hockey, and individual sports such as gymnastics, tennis, and swimming).

We received responses from children who played a variety of sports, including baseball, basketball, soccer, ice hockey, football, and swimming. Most had played some of the sports for only a season or two, while others had played some sports for eight to nine years.

Positives about Youth Sports

The first question we asked was: "What three things do you

like best about playing in organized youth sport?" We got a variety of responses, as you might expect, but the most frequent reasons mentioned were making new friends—"I like meeting new people" and "You can make new friends"—and reaffirming current friendships—"I get to play with my friends" and "I like having a great time and being with my friends." Not far behind was the idea of having fun—"It's fun." Developing skills was frequently mentioned: "I get to learn more about the sport" and "Constantly learning how to play well." Challenge and competition were also frequently cited—"I like the challenge" and "Competition—I like to compete. I like to push myself."

Negatives about Youth Sports

The next question, of course, addressed "What three things do you like least about playing in organized youth sport?" There were many different responses to this question as well. At the top of the list was pressure—"Pressure from other people," "Too much pressure to win," and "Sometimes you are pressured or you can't play because the coach is too worried about winning." The coach was often singled out for criticism— "Some coaches take it too seriously—they work you too hard, they make it not fun" and "Coaches take it too seriously and yell at the kids."

Embarrassment appeared in some cases—"Parents run around screaming, 'That kid's mine, that kid's mine,'" but more often pressure from parents was noted—"Getting pushed to win by my parents (when I win I get presents, when I lose I get nothing)." Parental behavior is an issue for many, as in "Having other teams' parents yelling at our parents" and "Parents on the other team boo your team." It's hard to believe that parents would do that, but it happens! And if it's not the other team, it may be your team—"Sometimes the parents get out of control and start yelling at the kids." The negative side of parental involvement by some parents was further expressed in "Unsportsmanlike conduct by parents" and "Unruly parents." Perhaps these are some parents you know (and perhaps they would benefit from reading this book!). A few youngsters were perceptive enough to note the political side of youth sports—"League and club politics," "I don't like the politics," and "The leaders only care about making parents happy."

How to Improve Things

Thinking that sometimes kids do know best, we asked the youngsters this: "If you had the power to change some things in the organized youth sport setting(s) in which you play, what would they be and how would you change them?" While some of the answers were more schedule-oriented—"I'd change the hours you had to practice if it's early in the morning" (Many of us would not be terribly excited about early morning practices either), or rule-based—"No walk in baseball—bat until you get a hit," there were quite a few responses that addressed behavior of parents and leagues.

One child thought, "There are too many adults involved and it is too organized. Kids need to be free." Another child didn't mince words—"I would like better refs and for parents not to all think their kids are all going to be pros. And to offer nice encouragement, but for the most part, at least during the game, keep their mouths shut!" Coaches were singled out in two cases—"Nicer coaches—I would let the kids elect the coach they want" and "The coaches have to sit in the dugout and not curse off the umpires." One youngster even suggested that "I would like to have kids on the board to make some of the decisions on what goes on in that sport, because the kids are the ones that play." Now that is a great idea!

Parents do good things!

Focusing on parents specifically, we next asked: "What kinds of things do you see parents of youngsters who play in organized youth sport setting(s) do that you think are good?" It was exciting to hear that parents do many good things. Some responses indicated that: "Parents encourage their children" and "I see the parents motivating and telling the kids how good they are doing and cheering them on." Others said: "I like the way they give support whether you had a good or bad game" and "They cheer for the teams playing. They support their kids. They put lots of time and money into their kids playing sports." Children do recognize the sacrifice of time and money that parents do put in— "Give their children positive support, provide support for the team, and provide their child with necessities to play the game." And there's always the draw of McDonald's, Pizza Hut, or Baskin Robbins—"Take you out after the game to eat."

The idea of not putting on pressure came up often—"Correct errors—It's good when they are just being helpful and not putting on the pressure. They're giving encouragement, like when they say 'Good hustling,' " and "When parents are encouraging by saying, 'Try your best,' not putting pressure on us." Support at all times is critical—"Parents should cheer for kids if they do good, but shouldn't boo if they do bad," and "Well, they encourage the youngster to do the best they can while giving 110%. They believe that winning is not everything, but it sure helps. They encourage their youngsters to be good sports." In the end, it is important to remember that it is your child's game—"I see parents letting the children make their own decisions and just letting them play the game."

Parents do bad things!

Having asked about the good things that parents do, we had

to also ask "What kinds of things do you see parents of young-sters who play in organized youth sport setting(s) do that you think are bad?" There were, as expected, many negative things that parents do. Perhaps you see some people you know in these comments, or even yourself!

Yelling seems to be a big part of some parents' behavior—"I see the parents yelling, swearing, and telling them how bad they are doing when the kids don't need to hear all of that" and "On occasion I see some parents yelling or giving their children or other players bad looks." Another example offered was "I think some parents set bad examples for and sometimes embarrass their kids by *constantly* screaming at the refs, coaches, players on other teams and other parents. Also, if a player makes a mis-take or misses a shot or pass, etc., they don't need to have it all rerun after the game by the parents." One youngster noted that: "They are too hard on their kids. They yell at the kids and refer-ees when they get mad. They don't just come to the game to watch, they start yelling." Another child said that: "I hate it when they 'just yell at us' without offering encouragement."

Pressure also seems to be a constant source of conflict. Re-sponses such as "Sometimes I see that they are pushing them too much. It is fine if the kid wants it as bad, but if they do not, it is bad. The kids feel the pressure on them, forcing them to play bad." Other youngsters said that: "They [parents] get down too hard on their kids" and "Some parents take the game way too seriously and make the kids not want to play because they are on their case all the time." Several more responses indicated that: "Some say bad things to their kids. Parents are too con-cerned with winning," and "Angry at kids when the team loses. Angry at kids for making a mistake." Finally, one youngster said that: "Parents can be too hard on their kids, they expect too much from the team, and they overly criticize the coach."

Some parents don't make it in the role model category— "When I see a parent playing the sport, ice hockey, I see bad events that occur in the game, such as fighting, bad language, etc.," and "All the cursing, and being bad sports about it." Have you seen/heard any parents in this category?—"Once during a hockey game, I heard one of the parents yelling to their son from the stands to play dirty. No matter what the game might be, there is always at least one set of parents yelling from the stands." One response combined a few of the above points: "Some bad things that parents do that drive me crazy are fight with the other parents from the other team, pushing kids so much, until the child decides to quit by themselves because they can't take the pressure."

One child perceptively noted the importance of keeping the team in mind if it is a team sport: "I don't like parents that are only there to support their child and only work for their child's benefit. Because it is a team." In the end one bit of advice may be helpful—"I wish they'd just leave us alone to play."

Advice—Words of Wisdom to Guide our Behavior

We wanted, in the end, to get some advice from our children about what we can do—"What advice would you give parents of youngsters who play in organized youth sport setting(s)?" Many of the suggestions were excellent:

"I would tell them to encourage their children, not be too hard on them and have fun."

"The advice I would give parents is come watch the games, cheer for both teams, not yell at your kids, and just enjoy watching them play."

"Remember you aren't the one playing and not to go overboard with criticism. Remember—they are your kids and it's a game."

"Let their kids play their own game."

"I don't think it is for them to worry whether their son excels in a sport. I think if they have made their son/daughter happy with what they're doing, they should be satisfied."

"Just tell your kids to play hard and mostly have fun. Tell them to listen to their coaches."

"Don't interfere with the coach during the game. Keep comments positive and supportive to *all* kids on the team, especially their own. Don't be a sore loser. Make sure the game is always *fun* for your kid."

"Support their kid and cheer him on when they do something good, but don't yell at them when they make an error."

"Just let the kids play the game to have them do their best and let the coaches do the coaching."

"Don't worry—let the kids enjoy the game."

"Keep encouraging us and telling us to be the best we can be."

"Don't come to the practices. Don't pressure us. Just let the kids 'be all they can be.'"

"Don't choose the sport for the kids. If a kid hates the pool, they won't like swimming. If a kid hates to run, they won't like soccer. And don't pay for it—enrollment—first and then tell the kid he has to go/stay. I chose swimming at first because my friends were there. Then I stayed because I was doing well at it."

"Help your kids if they ask for it. Don't force them to do anything that they don't want to do. Be a spectator, not a coach."

"Shut up, sit down, watch the game quietly, and let your kid have fun."

"I would tell these parents to encourage their children and to have them give 100%, but not to push them too hard. Also, when they go to games they should cheer the child on, but not get so excited they fight with other parents. That's crazy!"

"Cheer for your team. Don't boo kids. If your kid does bad make him feel good. Point out the good things they did."

"Just believe in your kids. Urge them to win, but then if they do not win, it is all right also."

"Encourage them and be positive. Tell them that we're out to have fun and we don't care that much about winning."

"The advice I would give parents would be to just come to the games and enjoy them. Don't be so hard on their kids. Cheer for both teams if something good happens. Treasure your kids for what they are, not for what you want them to be."

Summary

The message is often more powerful when it comes from our children. These young sports participants have said, in their own words, much of what we have suggested in our earlier chapters. The key elements of their message are presented in the next chapter, Chapter 8, which is for your children to read and use in their relationships with you, their parents. It is up to us, as parents, to *listen* to what our children are telling us, that it is their game to play and enjoy!

Chapter 8

Our Children—
Your Chapter

PARENTS: Please give this chapter to your children to read (and please read it yourself as well)—it is our / your message to them about what this book is all about.

This book is called *The Total Sports Experience—for Kids: A Parent's Guide to Success in Youth Sports.* Most of this book is for your parents, but we wanted to write a chapter for you, our children. We have some suggestions for *you* in helping *us*, your parents, help *you* get the most out of sports and be as successful as you can be.

What Is Success?

First, what is success? Success can mean many things. We believe that success is doing the very best you can. Success means trying your hardest in each practice and each competition. It means never giving up on yourself and your teammates. Success means giving it everything you can. Success is *not* about winning. You know that. Some parents don't know that. Some parents are more concerned with the final score than how you played. You have to help us teach these parents. You have to help these parents learn what is the most important for you.

Our Children—Your Chapter

It can be very disappointing when you lose a big match or a tournament. But losing a game does not mean you are a loser. Losing a game just means you didn't win that day. You are successful if you walk away knowing you gave it your best. That's the most important thing!

Second, what is sports all about? Sports is about having fun, about being physically active, about playing with your friends (and making new friends), about learning new skills, about becoming a better player and a better person. You play sports for many reasons. Some of you play to compete and win, and that's okay! But we hope that the most important reason you play now, and will play sports for the rest of your life (even if the sports change), is to have fun. If it's not fun, change it so it is fun. And if someone (like coaches, parents, or friends) is not making it fun, then talk to someone who can help change what is going on or can get you into a program that is fun. You may even be able to change the way they think about sports, because sports should be fun. You should enjoy what you do!

What can you do with your parents to help them understand how you want them to behave? The first thing you can do is give them a copy of the Bill of Rights for Youth Sports (see Appendix 2). We believe in it and think you will too. Ask your parents to read it and agree with you that they will support it. If you help your parents understand what you really want in your game, perhaps they will listen and understand. Help them realize that you want them to share in the joy of your game.

The second thing you can do is talk with your parents. For example, do your parents know what you like and don't like about playing sports? What things can you tell your parents? Here is a list of four things we think you can tell your parents. Talk with them if they don't understand what you mean. Hopefully your parents already do these things! If not, give them a chance to think about what you are telling them—even though they are older than you, they can still learn something new.

1. Tell your parents why you like to play sports. We asked other children why they like to play sports, and they said they liked to play because sports are fun, they like to play with their friends (and make new friends), and they like to learn how to play sports better. You may have some other reasons why you play. The important thing is to tell your parents why you like to play sports.

2. Tell your parents about the good things they do. We asked other children about some of the good things that parents do. They said they liked it when parents encouraged them. They liked it when parents supported them if they had a good game or a bad game. They liked it when parents cheered for them. They liked it when parents let them make their own decisions and let them play. You may have other things you think are good. The important thing is to let your parents know about the good things they do and other parents do.

3. Tell your parents what you don't like about playing sports. We asked other children what they don't like about playing sports, and they said they didn't like all the pressure they got, from parents and coaches. They didn't like it when their parents (and coaches) yelled at them. They didn't like it when their parents behaved badly, like yelling at the other team or even getting into fights sometimes. You may have other things you don't like. The important thing is to tell your parents what you don't like. When we asked other children to *tell us about the bad things that parents do*, they told us the same things that they didn't like about playing sports. The important thing is to let your parents know about the bad things they do and other parents do.

4. How to make things better. Tell your parents to read and support the Bill of Rights. Tell your parents to do these five things:

"I can"

Let me have fun—Help make playing sports fun.

Encourage me—Encourage me and support me—I'm the one who is playing and I like to know you like that. Don't put pressure on me.

Cheer for me and all the other players.

Teach me—show me how to behave and how to play the right way. Show me how to be a good sport.

Believe in me—I am trying as hard as I can. Let me have fun and do my best—that is all you can ask for and that is all I can do.

enjoyment

You can help your parents help you be a success in sports. Talk with your parents. Tell them when they do good things. Tell them you like that. Tell them when they do bad things or things that make you uncomfortable. Tell them you don't like that. They will support you and believe in you. Remember, the most important thing—*have fun!*

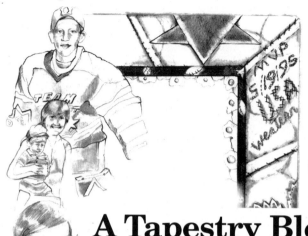

A Tapestry Blended of Many Colors:
Putting It All Together

Like an album of yellowed family photographs, memories of our children in sports will remind us of wonderful times in our life. These early life experiences will represent a personal anthology, rich with history, joy, excitement and, perhaps, moments of sadness and disappointment. As parents, how can we capture the essence of our past? What can we do to encapsulate all those years and preserve the integrity of our memories?

We have tried to provide you with an overview of the meaning of sports in your children's lives and how you can be supportive of them while they are involved in sports. More importantly, we hope we have given you a foundation which kindles a more kindhearted point of view about youth sports.

Throughout the book, one of our major goals has been to persuade you, as parents, that it is your children's game. Parents need to be more conscious of this and try not to take charge. We hope we have also provided you with a clear understanding of the value of sports and how, as parents, you can be most helpful to your children, both on the sidelines and at home.

A Tapestry Blended of Many Colors

As parents, we should not force our children to participate in any particular sport, but rather let our children make their own selections. It is crucial that children's involvement in organized sports be for *their* enjoyment. That must be the primary reason for their enrollment, at any age. If the fun is gone, they lose out.

This final chapter is our capstone, an integration of our thoughts, our reflections. The categories listed are not in any specific order of priority; rather, each of the points should be considered equally.

It is all about Fun!

As we highlighted throughout our journey, the aspect of fun is the most important ingredient in children's sports. In Chapter 7, where children identified their concerns, it was vividly clear that children of all ages consistently join because they enjoy what they do. The joy and challenges found in sports are often launching pads for new opportunities. As parents, we should not invade our children's world and take the fun out of their activities. We should never undermine the importance of fun to our children; when that occurs, a sense of emptiness develops. Even at high levels of competition, children still need to know that they can have fun.

Our main suggestion is to recognize this underlying desire for fun and not cheat children out of this opportunity. When children miss the fun of sports consistently, we will eventually find disheartened children. This may not be observable immediately, but eventually it will take its toll.

A wise person once said that happy people all seem to have something to look forward to in life. Perhaps that is what makes sports a journey well traveled during childhood.

It is all about Friendship and Camaraderie!

How many of us remember the days when all our friends

were either on the ballfield, or in the parks, the gyms or the rinks. Sports are about friendship and sharing a love of the game with another. It is a time when children should be children, and when laughter and tears are shared. Ask any adult about the sporting years and s/he will eventually begin to reminisce about the friends that were made.

Every year it has been the same in our homes. Teammates come over after games to celebrate the wins and to commiserate over the losses. Most of the time, the game is left at the park or the arena, but relationships continue to glow. Children need options in which they can meet new friends and share in childhood fun. Sport is all about relationships; some are short-lived while others last for a lifetime, a lifetime filled with treasures of memories of when we were able to glide, run, and play like the wind.

It is all about Choice!

As we stressed throughout the book, choice is a pivotal ingredient. Children must realize they can impact their own futures. They should not feel they are captive audiences whom we can register in activities in which they do not want to be involved. Choice promotes a sense of freedom and empowerment in children. Giving children a choice is definitely an important aspect in any leisure pursuit. Parents need to know their own children and understand individual differences, especially as it applies to younger children who may need a great deal of direction.

Choice not only represents the opportunity to select a given sport, but also the opportunity to be involved in selecting the level of expectations (e.g., competitive, cooperative, and elite levels) and other requirements. When children feel coerced or forced to take part in an activity, they may eventually want to give up. They need to know that their input will be respected.

It is all about Health and Physical Development!

Sports participation is a tremendous outlet to create a

healthy lifestyle. Participation in sports encourages children to recognize how important staying active is. It also reinforces a foundation early in life that promotes a healthy lifestyle. Children who are active in sports are more likely to include some of these activities later in their lives. However, what is important to children is that, while playing, they are exercising and revitalizing their bodies. This is especially important today when many children have become excessively dependent on electronic devices for their leisure (i.e., electronic games, computers, television).

We are more concerned now than ever before that many children are struggling with obesity and are not physically capable of vigorous activity. Perhaps this is due to our children not being active. Organized sports can contribute to physical and psychological well-being and should not be ignored. There are many options available, with varying levels of challenges for everyone.

It is all about Knowing Where to Start and Being Supportive!

We strongly recommend that all families understand the consequences of participating in youth sports. There are many options for children's involvement. What is important is that there needs to be a strategy in place. Parents and children should sit down and discuss the choices they have, including the level of competition, expectations, and commitments needed. It is important for the child to be the major decision maker whenever possible.

The home atmosphere must be supportive for children to excel and enjoy their sporting lives. Parents should applaud good effort in both victory and defeat. Parents must recognize that they should not shout or mentally abuse a child after games or practices. These reactions will only be destructive in the end.

It is all about Knowing Your Rights and Your Children's Rights!

There are many elements in this dimension. It represents parental commitment in teaching and assisting our children in developing the necessary skills to compete and play. Inherent in this position is our steadfast commitment that parents must continue to be encouraging.

Within this category, how much control should we give to coaches and lay leaders in their interactions with and influence on our young children? At what point do we openly question the style of interaction they select in working with our children? We noted the dimension of communication is vital. Some children are sensitive to harsh feedback and would adapt better with a different approach. It is our challenge to get that information acknowledged or understood by the coaching staff.

We must recognize that we should be more outspoken if we see a coach mentally abusing children or being excessively harsh. However, we also must realize that at different ages the expectations and the manner in which coaches interact with children will change tremendously. We must proceed with guided caution. It is always helpful for parents to develop small, informal networks so that they can talk to other families and learn how they contend with difficulties.

Verbal and mental abuse are never acceptable, but different coaching styles may come across more "forcefully" than others—know the context in which the questionable interaction has taken place and act accordingly. After reviewing the options, parents should not be neglectful and allow their children or the children of others to be abused. For example, should we be accepting of a coach who is very harsh, unfair, and abrupt in interacting with our child? In the heat of the moment, we may not realize that we should be concerned in the long run with our children's investment in sports. One terrible coaching experiencing can turn a child off for a lifetime.

Children do not need to be treated badly, especially when the approaches of coaches and others may not be in the style in which we respond to our children. For example, we have all seen coaches who are sometimes very rude and abrupt. Developmentally, some children are more capable of coping with these actions than others. Young children do not need these negative reactions and, as parents, we must safeguard their rights.

The Bill of Rights for Young Athletes (see Appendix 2) is important in providing an underlying philosophy for our (and hopefully your) approach to youth sports. It would be great if your child's coach and the other children's families agreed with this philosophy and adopted it as their standard as well.

It is all about Being a Good Sport and Not Making a Fool of Yourself!

This goes for both parents and children. Over their sporting years, we should all hope to inspire our children to develop a sense of good sportsmanship and tolerance. However, children learn from their surroundings. As adults, we must take control of our own behavior. Remember, it is only a game!

Only a few days ago, we were talking to a 12-year-old child who is truly a wonderful baseball player. He has recently begun to struggle and feel demoralized. He seems to have difficulty blocking out the shouting from the fans who razz him when he goes up to bat. Sure, they came to cheer the other team, but why do some fans have to go out of their way to be objectionable? Remember, do unto others as you would have done unto you. If you do not want to cheer for the other team, that is fine; nevertheless, we should not be intentionally harsh to any other children just because they are on another team. The children on the other team have parents, who, we hope, will treat our child with respect.

Children are sometimes embarrassed by their parents. As guests, we should act accordingly. None of us wish to make fools of ourselves. It is not our right to be mean-spirited, because children eventually will follow our examples. More importantly, we should really not misbehave because it is not our game!

It is all about Communication!

Communication means many things. It can be defined as expressing thoughts through dialogue. However, we mean many other things when we talk about communication.

First, communication represents a clear understanding of the expectations and values of all parties involved. What are the goals and objectives of a particular league? Have allowances been made for the differences between more competitive and more cooperative programs? How do the leagues handle children with individual differences and what are their guidelines for participation?

Second, communication represents a network of connections among the values and expectations of a league, the coaches, the parents, and the children. It is important for families to make sure there is consistency between what is promised and what is actually delivered. Any member of this informal network should be able to clarify concerns and try to work them out.

Finally, communication at the basic level represents the interaction among the children, teammates, coaches, and parents. Provisions need to be made so that concerns can be worked out before they grow into disasters. Children and families need to feel comfortable that they can solve problems in a forum that is accepting of feedback. This requires a willingness to communicate. We have seen many good teams fall apart because they did not have the willingness to work things through. Sometimes it is not the coaches who are obstructing the solution, but rather the parents. In the end, it is the children who pay for the selfishness and lack of insight on the part of the adults.

It is all about Listening to Our Children!

We have emphasized that parents must listen to their children. We have to listen not only to what is said, but also to what may not be said. We started by saying that parents need to pay attention to what a child is saying about a sport. That is the first step. If the children say they are interested, then we should proceed, but if they are resistant, we need to know not to push. There are times when parents know that a child may really mean yes, but needs some prodding. If a child says no, that does not mean it is no forever. Parents may want to revisit the opportunity at a different time and not close the door.

Listening also means being aware of how a child is handling the challenges inherent in sports. Parents should listen to make sure that the child is coping with and enjoying the experience. When a child returns from a practice or a game, parents should be patient and allow the child to get things off his or her chest. It is amazing what may come out if we are patient.

Parents must recognize that the drive to and from can be a valuable opportunity for children to share feelings and experiences. However, parents need to attempt to set the atmosphere so it is conducive to listening. This includes not aggressively questioning the child, but rather giving the child a chance to talk. It also includes making sure that the child knows you want to listen. Those short drives can be soothing and optimal for relationship building.

Finally, listening also incorporates trying to be perceptive and ascertaining whether there is something the child is not talking about. Parents should be observant and try to determine whether they can be helpful before being asked. Children find it wonderful to be helped before they ask.

It is all about Knowing How to Motivate and Encourage Your Child!

Families would benefit from understanding Psychological Skills Training and how to apply some of the basic strategies at home. Knowing how to set the stage at home will promote a healthier mental state for your child. It will potentially prepare your child to play games.

Along with knowing how to apply some psychological skills, parents should recognize what potentially motivates or discourages their children. As discussed in the chapter on self-esteem, there are many ingredients to healthy self-esteem. As parents, we should try to emulate positive coping strategies at home (e.g., healthy self-talk) and help our children develop manners that promote a positive outlook.

Parents should try to understand how some of the theories we discussed actually apply in their daily lives. For example, is the child an individual who is success-driven or failure-avoiding? Understanding this perception may explain what motivates the child. An individual who is more apt to be success-driven will be more willing to take risks and will be more accepting of failure. Remember, we have to demonstrate to our children that failure is an event, not a person. Children can learn that they can prevail if they don't give up.

Last, but not least, you know a great deal about your children. It is imperative that parents provide the insight they have to coaches and lay individuals. This information may be very helpful in supporting the child. This also includes giving input on how the coaching staff can best deal with any behavioral and/ or medical conditions that a child may have. Some parents may be apprehensive about sharing information because of concerns that the information given may affect the child's involvement.

Nevertheless, if we see a child struggling because of a lack of understanding, we need to close that information gap. It can potentially resolve many future challenges.

It is all about Valuing a Small Window of Time!

All along, we have supported the position that, as parents, we must cherish what we have today, because in an eye-blink of time these events will be gone. As parents, we must make a conscious effort to appreciate what we have. An analogy would be putting together all our memories (good and bad) into some sort of mental or physical scrapbook so we can capture childhood for a lifetime. The notion of a small window of time does not ignore that we are still in the driver's seat and can always alter the route or change the destination.

It is all about Appreciating the Present and Not Dwelling on the Future!

Too many parents see sports as an avenue to future employment and opportunities. A small percentage of children do go on to become professional athletes and Olympians, but this is not true for most! Parents should not dwell on how they can plan the future, but rather on how sports activities enrich childhood.

If the opportunities make themselves available, and the child can earn a scholarship or even become a professional, then all the better. However, if we put pressure on our children to excel because of those reasons, will they feel neglected and overwhelmed? We have even heard of parents who put small transmitters in a child's helmet so they could communicate with the child on the field! Most likely, the coaching tips transmitted were not encouraging, but critical.

Parents need to recognize how hard they can actually push (try to influence) a child. This usually involves parents realistically assessing the child's age, character, abilities, and willingness to accept challenges and responsibilities. This should take the form of encouragement, not pressure.

It is all about Putting Youth and Sports into Proper Perspective!

This principle is, in many ways, the most crucial. It integrates the most important elements noted in each of the principles discussed thus far. Our perspective should begin with an awareness of limited time. For most children, the adventure with organized sports will eventually end. Families must realize this and try to enjoy what they have, rather than what they do not have. This does not mean that we do not continue to encourage our children to excel, or to help our children find the best matches with their talents, levels of competitiveness and emotionally stability; rather, it suggests that at each time period, parents should take in the values of sports and enjoy watching and being participants.

Parents must appreciate their children with all their sporting limitations. It is easier to modify or move obstructions when you are pushing with the grain than against it. What is wonderful is that all children have treasures, but for some we may have to dig around to help them unearth their assets.

Parents must remember that life is a journey ready for exploration. We must appreciate what we have before it is gone. We hope that every one of us will take the time to go slowly enough on our journeys so that we do not miss any of the sights. Rushing and ignoring the little details will alter our perceptions of our journeys. Two families could take off on the same day for exactly the same destination, and what they remember and see when they return will be vastly different. Individual differences are expected, but we should all try to enjoy the journey and "smell the flowers along the way."

It is all about Watching Your Child Grow Up and "REMEMBERING WHEN"!

In the end, a package of memories is the legacy that we will take with us. The pictures, videos, and trophies are the mementos of the years gone by. These mementos will make it easier for reminiscing and capturing the true spirit of our memories. When we stop and think about it, some of our readers are just beginning their carousel ride with sports while for others it is about to end. Although the eras may differ (watching your young child play for the first time versus the veteran), some parents view the game with the same zest with which they began. They are just proud to be part of this extraordinary time in a child's life. Many of us will continue to sparkle because it does not really matter how old our children are. They are still our children.

There may be periods when we will pass major milestones. Teams that have been together for years may begin to dissolve (due to age and new interests) or children's interests will just change. These are times that will be more special because they represent a child's celebration of coming of age. Perhaps some of you can even visualize, right at this second, a wonderful moment, and try to capture the reflection.

In the end, it will be the little things that most of us will remember with fondness. Our reflections will not center on all the games our child has won, nor the all-star teams for which he or she was or was not selected, nor the trophies that were garnered. Rather, we will simply remember when.

What is wonderful is that, for each of us, the memories will be quite different. We may package them developmentally in our minds, making it easier to select highlights of various episodes that were important to our children. The memories will be special, not only because of what they were but what they represent—segments of our children's life histories.

Some families may even find themselves becoming emotional when an era is about to end. Both of us have had this experience. It seems amazing that, although we can not truly gauge them, the years just seem to go by. When most families become involved with sports, the children need our help. Now, they are just glad that their parents take a strong interest and are involved.

As parents, we must try to do the best we can. Over the years, if we provide our children with the support, guidance, respect, and love they deserve, our experiences with sports should be very positive. As we said at the beginning, "Treat your memories and life experiences as you do your pictures and place them in their best light in your mind forever. The pictures that are enshrined in your mind can always be there even if the episodes, events, activities and places are not." Having had the opportunity to share your child's game will be a treasure that you will cherish for your entire lifetime. That is what parenting is all about: sharing our love through life with our children.

Developmental Expectations of Various Sports Years

Early Childhood School-Age (3-6)

Motor
• Large muscle, basic motor skills acquired rapidly.
• Skills developing, but at different rates for different children.
• Strength increases rapidly.
• Increased coordination and balance development.
• High energy level (especially for short periods of time).

Cognitive
• Thinking at this age is generally intuitive and illogical.
• The child focuses on salient perceptual features of the world and often ignores other relevant information.

Emotional
• The child attempts to become more assertive and independent in his or her development.
• Children try to exercise their own initiative and need to be guided.

• The child of 5-6 believes that rules about how to play or about how to behave are absolute and can not be changed. When rules are broken, a child at this age believes the punishment should be based on how much damage was done, not by the intentions of the child.

• Friendships are very basic. At this age, the young child considers the children s/he plays with as friends. Friendships can begin and end quickly on acts of kindness or, for that matter, meanness.

Implications

• Love for movement exploration
• Creative, imaginative
• Individualistic
• Love for singing, rhythm
• Beginning of learning to share, parallel play
• Focus on cooperation (not competition)

The School-Age Child (6-12)

Motor

• Balance develops more fully.
• Basic motor patterns become more refined.
• Coordination and body control improve.
• Strength and endurance increase.
• Eye-hand coordination improves.
• Attention span increases.
• Improvements in all areas of motor fitness year by year—coordination, balance, speed, agility, and power.

Cognitive

• This stage marks the advent of what is considered operational thinking.
• A major accomplishment of this stage is the ability to conserve.

• A limitation is that thinking is primarily at a concrete level.

Emotional

• The child is confronted with new expectations and being constantly compared with others.

• Children of this age genuinely enter the competitive world and find themselves learning new skills and having to become industrious.

• Those who frequently encounter failures potentially risk developing a sense of inferiority and incompetence.

• As children begin to interact more with their peers, they come to realize that people make rules and therefore rules can be changed with discussions.

• Friendships at this age change tremendously.

• Friendships progress from play relationships based on immediate needs to that based on companionship.

• Children begin to base their choices of friends more on concrete and stable personal qualities.

• As children enter the school years, they begin to become more aware that others' feelings are separate from their own.

Implications

• Need to practice skills to improve acknowledged.
• Adventurousness increases.
• Social maturity develops/increases.
• Sense of group develops.
• Competitive spirit begins to develop.

Adolescence (13-18)

Motor

• Improvements in all areas of motor fitness—coordination, balance, speed, agility, and power, some of these areas may plateau for some adolescents.

Cognitive
• An individual in this stage can think abstractly and hypothetically.

Emotional
• Teenagers battle to achieve a sense of identity in regards to their gender roles, relationships with family members, and peers, as well as in their education.
• Identity refers to deliberate choices and decisions that teens make about many of the major issues that they are dealing with.
• Morally, teens are confronted in making numerous decisions which impact their lives.
• By late teen years, the young individuals should be capable of making advanced moral decisions based on abstract concepts of justice, dignity, and, for that matter, equality.
• Friendships at this age are viewed as those who share common interests and values.
• In the teen years, friends provide a strong psychological support system. Friendships appear to be more intricate as the teens age. Therefore, friendships are more difficult to break up in comparison to earlier childhood years.

Implications
• Attention span increases.
• Social maturity increases.
• Interest in skill development/refinement increases.
• Competitive spirit may increase considerably, particularly in sport participants.

Additional information on motor characteristics and implications may be obtained from:

Eckert, Helen M. (1987). *Motor development.* (3rd edition) Indianapolis, IN: Benchmark Press, Inc.

Appendix 2

Bill of Rights for Young Athletes

1. *The right to participate in sports.*

2. *The right to participate at a level commensurate with each child's developmental level.*

3. *The right to have qualified adult leadership.*

4. *The right to participate in safe and healthy environments.*

5. *The right of children to share in the leadership and decision-making of their sport participation.*

6. *The right to play as a child and not as an adult.*

7. *The right to proper preparation for participation in sports.*

8. *The right to an equal opportunity to strive for success.*

9. *The right to be treated with dignity.*

10. *The right to have fun in sports.*

Reprinted with permission from the National Association for Sport and Physical Education, 1900 Association Drive, Reston, VA 20191.

Appendix 3

Resources for Parents

Some good applied sport psychology books for starters:

Martens, Rainer. (1987). *Coaches guide to sport psychology.* Champaign, IL: Human Kinetics Publishers.

Orlick, Terry. (1990). *In pursuit of excellence: How to win in sport and life through mental training.* (2nd Ed.) Champaign, IL: Human Kinetics Publishers.

Orlick, Terry. (1995). *Nice on my feelings: Nurturing the best in children and parents.* Carp, Ontario, Canada: Creative Bound.

Williams, Jean M. (Ed.) (1993). *Applied sport psychology: Personal growth to peak performance* (2nd ed.). Palo Alto, CA: Mayfield.

Some other books on youth sports that may provide additional helpful information:

American Sport Education Program. (1994). *SportParent.* Champaign, IL: Human Kinetics.

Appendix 3

Burnett, Darrell J. (1993). *Youth sports & self-esteem: A guide for parents*. Indianapolis, IN: Masters Press.

Cahill, Bernard R. & Pearl, Arthur J. (1993). *Intensive participation in children's sports*. Champaign, IL: Human Kinetics.

Fortanasce, Vincent M. (1995). *Life lessons from Little League: A guide for parents and coaches*. New York: Image/Doubleday.

Micheli, Lyle J. (1990). *Sportswise: An essential guide for young athletes, parents, and coaches*. Boston: Houghton Mifflin Company.

Rotella, Robert J., & Bunker, Linda K. (1987). *Parenting your superstar: How to help your child get the most out of sports*. Champaign, IL: Leisure Press.

Smith, Nathan J., Smith, Ronald E., & Smoll, Frank L. (1983). *Kidsports: A survival guide for parents*. Reading, MA: Addison-Wesley Publishing Company.

Smith, Ronald E., & Smoll, Frank L. (1996). *Way to go, coach:A scientifically-proven approach to coaching effectiveness*. Portola Valley, CA: Warde.

Smoll, Frank L., & Smith, Ronald E. (1995). *Children and youth in sport: A biopsychosocial perspective*. Dubuque, IA: Brown and Benchmark.

Smoll, Frank L., & Smith, Ronald E. (1996). *Coaches who never lose: A 30-minute primer for coaching effectiveness*. Portola Valley, CA: Warde.

Wolff, Rick. (1993). *Good sports*. New York: Dell.

Zulewski, Richard. (1994). *The parent's guide to coaching physically challenged children.* Cincinnati, OH: Betterway Books.

There are also some sport specific books available, such as Coaching Youth Baseball, a publication of the American Sport Education Program (ASEP)—see below. You can find some of these in your local bookstore, library, or through some of the organizations which follow.

A great place to contact for resources on sports in general, and youth sports in particular, is the Sport Information Resource Centre, which publishes SportDiscus, the premier online and CD-ROM computerized sport information data base.

Sport Information Resource Centre
1600 James Naismith Drive
Gloucester, Ontario, Canada K1B 5N4
telephone: (613) 748-5658
1-800-665-6413
fax: (613) 748-5701
e-mail: moreinfo@sirc.ca
WWW sites: http://www.sirc.ca
            http://www.SPORTQuest.com

Some places to call for coaching certification and training information:

American Sport Education Program
P.O. Box 5076
Champaign, IL 61825-5076
telephone: (217) 351-5076
1-800-747-5698
fax: (217) 351-2674
e-mail: asep@hkusa.com
WWW site: http://www.humankinetics.com

Appendix 3

Coaching Association of Canada
1600 James Naismith Drive
Gloucester, Ontario, Canada K1B 5N4
telephone: (613) 748-5624
fax: (613) 748-5707
e-mail: coach@coach.ca
WWW site: http://www.coach.ca

National Association for Girls and Women in Sport (NAGWS)
1900 Association Drive
Reston, VA 20191
telephone: (703) 476-3450
fax: (703) 476-9527
e-mail: NAGWS@AAHPERD.ORG
WWW site: http://www.aahperd.org/nagws.html

National Association for Sport and Physical Education (NASPE)
1900 Association Drive
Reston, VA 20191
telephone: (703) 476-3410
fax: (703) 476-8316
e-mail: NASPE@AAHPERD.ORG
WWW site: http://www.aahperd.org/naspe.html

National Youth Sport Coaches Association (NYSCA)
a division of the National Alliance for Youth Sports (NAYS)
2050 Vista Parkway
West Palm Beach, FL 33411
telephone: (407) 684-1141
1-800-729-2057
fax: (561) 684-2546
WWW site: http://www.nays.org

Performance Enhancement Services
contact person: Frank L. Smoll, Ph.D., Co-Director
telephone: (206) 543-4612
(see book listing for some of Frank Smoll and Ronald Smith's
recent publications)

Women's Sports Foundation
Eisenhower Park
East Meadow, NY 11554
telephone: (516) 542-4700
1-800-227-3988
fax: (516) 542-4716
e-mail: WoSport@aol.com
WWW site: http://www.lifetimetv.com/wosport

Youth Sports Institute
IM Sports Circle,
Michigan State University,
East Lansing, MI 48824-1049
telephone: (517) 353-6689
fax: (517) 353-5363
e-mail: ythsprts@msu.edu
WWW site: http://www.educ.msu.edu/units/dept/pees/ysi/
    ysihome. html
The Youth Sports Institute is the developer of the PACE pro-
gram mentioned in Chapter 5.)

Appendix 3

Some national organizations for major sports (names of sports in bold) to call for further information:

Little League Baseball
P.O. Box 3485
Williamsport, PA 17701
telephone: (717) 326-1921
fax: (717) 326-1074
e-mail: publicrelations@littleleague.org
WWW site: http://www.littleleague.org

For baseball also note Babe Ruth Baseball/Softball, Pony Baseball/ Softball, and George Khoury Association of Baseball Leagues

Pop Warner Little Scholars, Inc. (Football and Cheerleading)
516 Middletown Blvd., Suite C-100
Langhorne, PA 19047
telephone: (215) 752-2691
fax: (215) 752-2879

United States Golf Association (USGA)
P.O. Box 708
Fair Hills, NJ 07931
telephone: (908) 234-2300
fax: (908) 234-9687
e-mail: usga@ix.netcom.com
WWW sites: http://www.usga.org
http://www.usopen.com

USA Hockey
4965 N. 30th Street
Colorado Springs, CO 80919
telephone: (719) 599-5500
1-800-566-3288
fax: (719) 599-5994
e-mail: raeb@usahockey.org
WWW sites: http://www.usahockey.com
             http://www.inlinehockey.com

American Youth Soccer Organization (AYSO)
5403 W. 138th Street
Hawthorne, CA 90250
telephone: (310) 643-6455
1-800-USA-AYSO
fax:(310) 643-5310
e-mail:jean@ayso.org
WWW site:http://www.soccer.org

U.S. Youth Soccer Association
899 Residential Drive, Suite 117
Richardson, TX 75081
telephone: (214) 235-4499
1-800-4SOCCER
fax: (214) 235-4480
e-mail:call 1-800 number to check
WWW site:call 1-800 number to check

Appendix 3

American Softball Association (ASA)
2801 NE 50th Street
Oklahoma City, OK 73111-7203
telephone: (405) 424-5266
fax: (405) 424-3855
e-mail: info@softball.org
WWW site: http://www.softball.org

United States Swimming (USS)
1 Olympic Plaza
Colorado Springs, CO 80909
telephone: (719) 578-4578
fax:(719) 578-4669
e-mail: swiminfo@rmi.net
WWW site: http://www.usswim.org

United States Tennis Association (USTA)
70 West Red Oak Lane
White Plains, NY 10604
telephone: (914) 696-7000
fax: (914) 696-7167
e-mail: nicoll@usta.com
WWW site: http://www.usopen.org

USA Wrestling
6155 Lehman Drive
Colorado Springs, CO 80918
telephone: (719) 598-8181
fax: (719) 598-9440
WWW site: http://www.usawrestling.org

Looking for other sports or other organizations? The Encyclopedia of Associations is in the reference section of almost all libraries, and has sports organizations for sports from acrobatics to wristwrestling. If you can't find what you're looking for in your area, check out some of the associations in the encyclopedia.

Associations for Athletes with Disabilities:

American Athletic Association for the Deaf
3607 Washington Boulevard, Suite 4
Ogden, UT 84403-1737
telephone: (801) 393-8710
TTY: (801) 393-7916
fax: (801) 393-2263
e-mail: aaadeaf@aol.com
WWW site: http://www.vii.com/wasatch/aaad.htm

Disabled Sports USA
451 Hungerford Drive, Suite 100
Rockville, MD 20850
telephone: (301) 217-0960
TTD: (301) 217-0963
fax: (301) 217-0968
e-mail: dsusa@dsusa.org
WWW site: http://www.dsusa.org

Special Olympics International
1325 G Street, N.W., Suite 500
Washington, D.C. 20005-3104
telephone: (202) 628-3630
fax: (202) 628-0200
e-mail: specialolympics@msn.com
WWW site: http://www.specialolympics.org

Appendix 3

United States Association of Blind Athletes
33 North Institute
Colorado Springs, CO 80903
telephone: (719) 630-0422
fax: (719) 630-0616
e-mail: usaba@usa.net
WWW site: http://www.ares.csd.net/&aspurloc/usaba/usaba.htm

United States Cerebral Palsy Athletic Association (USCPAA)
200 Harrison Avenue
Newport, RI 02840
telephone: (401) 848-2460
fax: (401) 848-5280
e-mail: uscpaa@mail.bbsnet.com
WWW site: http://www.uscpaa.org

United States Les Autres Sports Association
1475 West Gray, Suite 166
Houston, TX 77019-4926
telephone: (713) 521-3737

About the Authors

Dr. Aubrey H. Fine is a licensed psychologist who specializes in working with children and their families. He has been active in youth sports consultation for over a decade, and is presently a Full Professor in the School of Education and Integrative Studies at California State Polytechnic University in Pomona, California. In addition to his teaching, public speaking, clinical work, and consulting duties, Dr. Fine is also a regular contributor to and an associate editor for several journals prominent in the field of child psychology. This is his third book.

Dr. Aubrey H. Fine
School of Education and Integrative Studies
California State Polytechnic University
3801 West Temple Ave.
Pomona, CA 91768-4079
Telephone: (909) 869-2799
Fax: (909) 625-2397
E-mail: AFINE@LAEDU.LALC.K12.CA.US

Dr. Michael L. Sachs, also a licensed psychologist, is a Certified Consultant, Association for the Advancement of Applied Sport Psychology, as well as an Associate Professor in the Department of Physical Education at Temple University in Philadelphia, Pennsylvania. When he is not busy with teaching, consulting, and writing books, he can usually be found participating in or watching sports. This is his fourth book.

Dr. Michael L. Sachs
Associate Professor
Department of Physical Education, 048-00
Temple University
Philadelphia, PA 19122
Telephone: (215) 204-8718
Fax: (215) 204-8705
E-mail: MSACHS@VM.TEMPLE.EDU